GOD HAS SPOKEN

By the same author

'FUNDAMENTALISM' AND THE WORD OF GOD
EVANGELISM AND THE SOVEREIGNTY OF GOD
OUR LORD'S UNDERSTANDING OF THE LAW OF GOD
KNOWING GOD
I WANT TO BE A CHRISTIAN
UNDER GOD'S WORD
FOR MAN'S SAKE
FREEDOM, AUTHORITY AND SCRIPTURE
THE EVANGELICAL ANGLICAN IDENTITY PROBLEM
A KIND OF NOAH'S ARK?
GOD'S WORDS
KEEP IN STEP WITH THE SPIRIT
YOUR FATHER LOVES YOU
AMONG GOD'S GIANTS
A PASSION FOR HOLINESS
LAID BACK RELIGION?
GOD IN OUR MIDST
CONCISE THEOLOGY
THE SPIRIT WITHIN YOU (with A. M. Stibbs)
CHRISTIANITY THE TRUE HUMANISM
    (with Thomas Howard)
LUTHER'S BONDAGE OF THE WILL
    (translated, with O. R. Johnston)

GOD
HAS SPOKEN

REVELATION AND THE BIBLE

J. I. PACKER

Baker Books

A Division of Baker Book House Co.
Grand Rapids, Michigan 49516

© 1979 by J. I. Packer
New material © 1993 by J. I. Packer

First published in Great Britain 1965
by Hodder and Stoughton
Second edition 1979
Revised and enlarged edition 1993
First Baker edition published in 1988
Second Baker revised and enlarged edition 1994

Published by Baker Books
a division of Baker Book House Company
P.O. Box 6287, Grand Rapids, MI 49516-6287

ISBN: 0-8010-7128-3

Printed in the United States of America

Other versions cited are the English Revised Version (E.R.V.) and the New English Bible (N.E.B.).

CONTENTS

To my colleagues at
Tyndale Hall and Trinity College, Bristol
1970–79
with affection and gratitude

FOREWORD (1993)

The older I get, the more I want to sing my faith and get others singing it with me. Theology, as I constantly tell my students, is for doxology: the first thing to do with it is to turn it into praise and thus honour the God who is its subject, the God in whose presence and by whose help it was worked out. Paul's summons to sing and make music in one's heart to the Lord is a word for theologians no less than for other people (Eph. 5:19). Theologies that cannot be sung (or prayed for that matter) are certainly wrong at a deep level, and such theologies leave me, in both senses, cold: cold-hearted and uninterested. I would think it tragic if this present book affected anyone like that.

I ask, therefore, that its contents, which are indeed theology, be received first and foremost as matter for praise, even though my argument is cast into the form of an extended sermon of a somewhat anxious kind. My main aim in these pages is to celebrate God's gift of revealed truth about Himself, through which we find fellowship with Him, receive salvation, and learn how to live. I should like the book to be understood as echoing and undergirding two hymns which I reproduce here for my readers' meditation. (The italics – need I say? – are mine.)

The first dates from 1953, twelve years before the first edition of this book. It runs thus:

> *God has spoken* – by his prophets,
> Spoken his unchanging word,
> Each from age to age proclaiming
> God the One, the righteous Lord:
> Mid the world's despair and turmoil
> One firm anchor still holds fast,

God is King, his throne eternal,
God the first and God the last.

God has spoken – by Christ Jesus,
Christ, the everlasting Son,
Brightness of the Father's glory,
With the Father ever one;
Spoken by the Word incarnate,
God of God, ere time began,
Light of Light, to earth descending,
Man, revealing God to man.

God yet speaks – his Holy Spirit
Speaks into the hearts of men,
In the age-long word expounding
God's own gospel, now as then;
Through the rise and fall of nations
One sure faith yet standing fast,
God abides, his word unchanging,
God the first and God the last.

The second hymn, written by Charles Wesley in the first flush of England's great evangelical awakening two and a half centuries ago, is better known.

O for a thousand tongues to sing
My great Redeemer's praise,
The glories of my God and King,
The triumphs of his grace!

Jesus – the name that charms our fears,
That bids our sorrows cease;
'Tis music in the sinner's ears;
'Tis life and health and peace.

He breaks the power of cancelled sin,
And sets the prisoner free:
His blood can make the foulest clean;
His blood availed for me.

He speaks; and, *listening to his voice*,
New life the dead receive;
The mournful, broken hearts rejoice;
The humble poor believe.

Hear him, ye deaf; his praise, ye dumb,
Your loosened tongues employ;
Ye blind, behold your Saviour come;
And leap, ye lame, for joy!

My gracious Master and my God,
Assist me to *proclaim*
And spread through all the earth abroad
The honours of thy name.

Let me say as plainly as I can that my goal in writing about the fact and process of revelation is to clear the path to a grasp of the realities that have been revealed – the knowledge of God, the Father, the Son, and the Holy Spirit, in creation, redemption, regeneration, and the upbuilding of the Church. Here are the wellsprings of Christian life, which preachers must spend their strength proclaiming, for the glory of God and the good of souls. Modern uncertainties about revelation have had the effect of damming the springs. It is my hope and prayer that this book might help to unblock them.

A book that has grown

A cat, says the proverb, may look at a king. Discerning readers will already have spotted that as I write this Foreword I have a king in my eye, one who may truly be called a king, namely John Calvin, who in the four books of the final edition of his *Institutes of the Christian Religion* dealt with creation, redemption, regenerate life and the Church, in that order, and whose passion for the glory and praise of God shone through every paragraph. In my role as observant cat, I feel some rapport with Calvin.

In the first place, I think the substance of this book would have his approval (look at *Inst.* I.i-ix and IV.viii.1-12 if you doubt me).

In the second place, it is a fact that Calvin's *Institutes* grew through five editions between 1536 and 1559 from a pocketbook on practical Christianity for general readership into a landmark treatise several times longer. This was mainly through the addition of relatively technical material relevant to the educating of preachers, material called forth in most cases by ongoing disagreements with what Calvin had originally offered. As a result, though he tried to keep everything at an educated layman's level, and to a remarkable extent succeeded, there are some rough gear changes as he moves from catechetical homiletic to theological apologetic and back again. I am somewhat in the same boat. *God has Spoken* began life in 1965 as a ninety-six-page paperback. It is now twice its original length, and the additions are mostly a degree more technical than the material to which they have been added. I can only ask my readers' indulgence, and state that I have tried hard to keep the style as simple as the argument allows.

Changes over thirty years

Although still, I believe, saying things of central relevance on a topic of central relevance, this basically 1965 book is now inevitably something of a period piece. It may ease the task of tuning in to it to note briefly three developments in the discussion of revelation and the Bible that make the 1993 scene different from that of 1965.

First, evangelical theology, of which this book is a sample product, is far stronger in the English-speaking world than it was a generation ago. The production of much written material of high quality to guide and support Bible-believers, and the scholarly work sponsored by the Tyndale Fellowship for Biblical Research (British), the Evangelical Theological Society (American), the International Council on Biblical Inerrancy during its decade of action (1977-87), and many publishers and theological colleges in addition, has given evangelical theology the status of a newly promising option, as distinct from that of a hopeless rearguard action, which is how it was widely rated in the 1950s and 1960s. When James Barr wrote his biggest book yet to attack evangelical scholarship as phoney and evangelical piety as pathological,[1] the most observable effect was to make his peers wonder what had happened to stir up in him so much anger and contempt: his jeremiad was not taken seriously, and his votes of censure were not seconded. I detect in *God has Spoken* a note of defiant defensiveness, especially in relation to the liberal theology that rode high in the England of the 1950s, as it had done for half a century before; but that tone would hardly be called for if I were writing from scratch today.

Second, the academic agenda in ongoing discussions about the Bible has shifted from revelation and inspiration to canon and hermeneutics, which means, in practical terms, interpretation. That is where most of the present-day action is, especially in North America, where the canonical (i.e. objective and organic) interpretation of Scripture that is maintained by the reformational forces, namely evangelicalism and biblical theology, stands in direct opposition to the selective, subjective hermeneutic of the various liberation theologies, most notably the feminist. As a discourse organized round the themes of revelation and inspiration, *God has Spoken* may therefore seem a bit old-fashioned, as Brahms does compared with Britten or Cliff Richard with Michael Jackson. However, clarity about revelation and inspiration is needed before canon and hermeneutics can be discussed to any good purpose, so the line of argument that this book develops is still, I believe, of fundamental importance. I have made some additions to the text to engage with these more recent interests, but revelation and inspiration continue to be my basic concerns.

Third, the main flow of the professional convictional stream among English-speaking theologians seems to have reversed itself. In place of the corporate assumption in what we may call the theologians' guild that constructive theology must embrace in some form the anti-supernatural unitarianism – deistic or pantheistic – of the Enlightenment, fresh delvings into Nicene trinitarianism, Chalcedonian incarnationalism,

and soteriology of an Athanasian or Augustinian sort have
become the accepted order of the day. The world of thought
to which *God has Spoken* belongs is thus no longer marginal,
as it seemed to be in 1965, when Bultmann, Tillich, John
Robinson and their camp-followers dominated the scene. It
is now centre stage. How long this reversal will last none
can say, but for the present, at least, listening to what the
Bible teaches about the three divine persons and the three
Rs of apostolic faith – ruin, redemption, and regeneration
– is less of an exotic oddity in the church than some of the
rhetoric in *God has Spoken* might suggest. I, for one, am very
thankful to God that this is so.

From my standpoint, then, some things have changed for
the better; but not by any means all. Classical Christian
theology, based on the classical Christian estimate of Scripture as the inspired Word of God, is still a minority position
in the older Protestant world on both sides of the Atlantic.
Arrogant teachers in schools and colleges are still trying to
beat out of young people any vestiges of evangelical belief
that they find in them. The tatters of a liberal establishment
remain in control of most of the mainline denominations
and of the World Council of Churches. The uncontrollable
relativism, pluralism, and ultimate nihilism, to which the
subjective method of liberal theology was bound sooner or
later to give rise, are currently being worked out in liberal and
radical circles as the terms 'God', 'Christ', 'faith' and 'love'
turn more and more into flexible noses of wax. The growing
pressure in the older churches to accept multi-faith syncretism
as a working principle, and to give a clean bill of health to
the homosexual lifestyle, are just two illustrations of this. The
thrust of *God has Spoken* is to reassert biblical authority and
the biblical method of living under that authority. I reissue the
book in the belief that the job it seeks to do is one that still
needs doing. May God use it to that end.

CHAPTER ONE

INTRODUCTION (1979)

The first version of this book was published in 1965, in a series called *Christian Foundations*. The series was by Anglicans for Anglicans, which is why so much Anglican matter was deployed in my text. The present revised and enlarged reissue is less specifically Anglican in its angle, though its demonstration of the Bible-based, Bible-oriented character of the Church of England formularies (the Thirty-nine Articles of 1563, the 1662 Book of Common Prayer, and the Homilies attested in Article 35) remains intact, as a testimony to my fellow-Anglicans of where their true roots are. Material from other traditions, is, however, freely used as well. Positions taken in 1965 are maintained, so far as I am aware, unchanged, but some of them are now amplified, illustrated and applied in a way that restrictions of length previously forbade.

My aim throughout is to prepare the minds of thinking Christian people to read and study their Bibles as Christians should. That aim determines both the contents and the spirit of what I now write.

ENJOYING YOUR BIBLE

A very helpful wayfarer's introduction to Bible study is John Blanchard's *Enjoy your Bible*. His title has a history: it belonged first to a book of a generation ago by the late G. Harding Wood, written to do essentially the same job, and it echoes the title of another fine book which went the rounds a generation before that, Harrington C. Lees' *The Joy of Bible Study* (1909). You see the emphasis: what is being highlighted is the prospect of pleasure through coming closer to the Scripture. And this emphasis is right. Pleasure, unalloyed and unending, is God's purpose for His people in every aspect and activity of their fellowship with Him. 'You will fill me with joy in your presence, with eternal pleasures at your right hand' (Ps. 16:11).

I hold the heady doctrine that no pleasures are so frequent or intense as those of the grateful, devoted, single-minded, whole-hearted, self-denying Christian. I maintain that the delights of work and leisure, of friendship and family, of eating and mating, of arts and crafts, of playing and watching games, of finding out and making things, of helping other people, and all the other noble pleasures that life affords, are doubled for the Christian; for, as the cheerful old Puritans used to say (no, sir, that is not a misprint, nor a Freudian lapse; I mean Puritans – the real, historical Puritans, as distinct from the smug sourpusses of last-century Anglo-American imagination), the Christian tastes God in all his or her pleasures, and this increases them, whereas for other people pleasure brings with it a sense of hollowness which reduces it. Also, I maintain that every encounter between the sincere Christian and God's word, 'the law from your mouth' (Ps. 119:72), however harrowing or humbling its import, brings joy as its spin-off, just as Blanchard, Wood and Lees imply, and the keener the Christian the greater the joy.

I know for myself what it is to enjoy the Bible – that is, to be glad at finding God and being found by Him in and through the Bible; I know by experience why the psalmist called God's message of promise and command his *delight* (Ps. 119:16, 24, 35, 47, 70, 77, 92, 143, 174 – nine times!) and his *joy* (vs. 111, cf. 14, 162; Ps. 19:8), and why he said that he *loved* it (Ps. 119:47, 48, 97, 113, 119, 127, 140, 159, 163, 167 – ten times!); I have proved, as have others, that as good food yields pleasure as well as nourishment, so does the good word of God. So I am all for Christians digging into their Bibles with expectations of enjoyment, and I applaud these writers for highlighting the prospect of joy to counter the common idea that Bible study is bound to be dry and dull. But for all that a balancing point needs, I think, to be made.

What is enjoyment? Essentially, it is a by-product: a contented, fulfilled state which comes from concentrating on something other than enjoying yourself. If enjoyment, as such, is your aim, you can expect to miss it, for you are disregarding the conditions of it. Pleasure-seeking, as we learn by experience, is a barren business; happiness is never found till we have the grace to stop looking for it, and to give our attention to persons and matters external to ourselves. In this case, Bible study will only give enjoyment if conforming to our Creator in belief and behaviour, through trust and obedience, is its goal. Bible study for our own pleasure rather than for God ends up giving pleasure neither to Him nor to us.

When Paul preached at Berea, the Jews there 'received the message with great eagerness and examined the Scriptures every day to see if what Paul said was true' (Acts 17:11). The 'word' was the message of salvation for lost mankind through Jesus Christ alone – 'there is no other name under heaven . . . by which we must be saved'; 'believe in the Lord Jesus, and you will be saved' (4:12, 16:31). The 'eagerness' sprang, no doubt, from a sense that each man's first need is to get clear on the issues of eternal destiny which the Gospel focuses and resolves. Such eagerness might nowadays be called 'existential concern', though 'eagerness' remains a clearer word for most people. The many Bereans who believed (Acts 17:12) doubtless testified afterwards to the joy of that spell of Bible study; what they undertook it for, however, was not joy as such, but certainty about God's way of salvation, and their joy came from finding what they sought – even though it must have cut across their previous ideas, and brought them a sense of sin and shame and helplessness that they had not known before. So for us: what brings joy is finding God's way, God's grace and God's fellowship through the Bible, even though again and again what the Bible says – that is, what God in the Bible tells us – knocks us flat.

Thus, the joy of Bible study is not the fun of collecting esoteric titbits about Gog and Magog, Tubal-cain and Methuselah, Bible numerics and the beast, and so on; nor is it the pleasure, intense for the tidy-minded, of analysing our translated text into preacher's pretty patterns, with neatly numbered headings held together by apt alliteration's artful aid. Rather, it is the deep contentment that comes of communing with the living Lord into whose presence the Bible takes us – a joy which only His own true disciples know.

SCRIPTURE AND SALVATION

In the last two paragraphs, as elsewhere in this book, I imply that our eternal destiny may depend on our attending to the Bible. In an age in which many do not attend to the Bible, some may find this implication at first blush incredible. So I had best come clean and face at once the question: do you really mean that? and are you really asking us to swallow it? The answer is yes, in the following sense.

First: in speaking of eternal destiny, I refer to that state of joy or grief beyond death of which I have learned from Jesus Christ, God's incarnate Son, who rose from the dead, and about which the authors of the New Testament, whom I take to be God-inspired and therefore worthy of trust, all agree. I am talking not of survival as such, but of a future state in which we consciously reap what we have actually sown. The New Testament makes plain that this life, in which bodies grow and wear out while characters get fixed, is an ante-chamber, dressing-room and moral gymnasium where, whether we know it or not, we all in fact prepare ourselves for a future life which will correspond for each of us to what we have chosen to be, and will have in it more of joy for some and distress for others than this world ever knows. 'For we must all appear before the judgment seat of Christ, that each one may receive what is due to him for the things done while in the body, whether good or bad' (2 Cor. 5:10).

Granted, secular fashion treats this life as the only life, and sees physical death as personal extinction, and cocks a snook at the notion of divine judgment. Granted, the self-absorbed passion for personal survival which pops up constantly in the modern West takes cranky and repellent forms. Granted, many Protestants (fewer Roman Catholics and Orthodox, to their credit) are so cowed by Marxist mockery of pie-in-the-sky-when-you-die, and so keen to string along with secular opinions, that they are no longer ready to tell anyone that life hereafter matters more than life here, and indeed they often themselves forget that this is actually so. (And what trouble that brings! Whenever God's providential programme of preparing us to enjoy Him hereafter proves to include physical or mental disability, cruelty or injustice from others, poverty, pain or deprivation – what the realistic old Puritans called 'losses and crosses' – these Protestants are at once bewildered and thrown off balance, and turn out to be pastorally useless; for, as Hebrews 12:1-14 shows, it is only by reference to the life to come that these things make sense.) Granted, too, exponents of biblical other-worldliness sometimes feed it into a funk-hole theology in which action for abolishing injustice, altering demonic power structures, controlling use of natural resources and reforming social evils is never a duty; and we cannot wonder if those who see these as obligatory concerns feel hostile to the doctrine which, as they think, teaches neglect of them. So anyone facing either the typical irreligion or the typical religion of the contemporary West might well feel uncertain and suspicious at any mention of the life beyond.

But wise persons will discount the emotional and reactionary element in their immediate thinking, and take seriously the sustained witness of Jesus and His apostles to the world to come, in which the abiding consequences of choices and commitments made here will be revealed and received. 'God "will give to each person according to what he has done". To those who by persistence in doing good seek glory, honour and immortality, he will give eternal life. But for those who . . . follow evil, there will be wrath and anger' (Rom. 2:6-8). Wise persons will keep in view this truth, which their own conscience will confirm to them if they let it speak, and will not let themselves fall victim to reactionary scepticism, even if others around them do so. Wise people know that reaction is never a sure guide to what is right and true.

Second: when I speak of attending to the Bible, I do so in terms of a distinction between its content, the message it embodies, and its outward form as a book now standing on your shelf or lying on your desk or by your bed. Having drawn the distinction, I can say at once that what determines our destiny is whether in our hearts we accept or reject the message of the Bible, and that message can be savingly received through liturgy, sermons, literature or conversations without ever reading the Bible for oneself. Christians who lived before the age of printed books, Christians who lived and died in illiteracy, and Roman Catholic Christians of the bad old days who were told that a vernacular Bible is a Protestant book, and lay study of it a Protestant vice which good Catholics eschew, and who believed this, but yet loved the Lord Jesus, are all proof of our point. God in His mercy will give understanding of His truth, knowledge of Christ and spiritual life, to any who sincerely seek Him, irrespective of the means by which His truth reaches them. So it is not absolutely necessary for salvation that one must read and study the biblical text. It would be gross superstition to think there is saving magic in the mere reading of the text where understanding and faith are lacking; it would be equally superstitious to suppose that God withholds grace from folk who know the Christian facts but, for whatever reason, fail to read the Bible for themselves.

Yet, as contemporary Roman Catholicism no less than historic Protestant evangelicalism knows and urges, one who fails to read the Bible is at an enormous disadvantage. Rightly are Bible reading and Bible-based meditation seen as prime means of grace. Not only is Scripture the fountain-head for knowledge of God, Christ and salvation, but it presents this knowledge in an incomparably vivid, powerful and evocative way. The canonical Scriptures are a veritable book of life, showing us God in relation to the most dramatic human crises (births, sicknesses, deaths, loves, losses, wars, falls, risks, disasters, failures, victories), the most elemental human emotions (joy, grief, love, hate, hope, fear, pain, anger, shame, awe) and the most basic human relationships (to parents, spouses, children, friends, neighbours, civil authorities, enemies, fellow-believers). Purely as man-to-man communication, simple, economical, imaginative, logical, Scripture is superb; it is no wonder that during the present century it has been the world's best-seller. On top of that, the fellowship of God with us humans to which it testifies is the most momentous reality we can ever know, and the power of the Bible in its readers' lives, a power springing both from its precious subject-matter and from its unique divine inspiration, is overwhelming.

The godly old Puritans called Scripture a 'cordial', meaning that it does for the soul what hot spirits do for the body, and everyone who reads the Bible seeking God finds this to be true. Scripture, which on the face of it is human witness to God, a compendium of sixty-six items put together over more than a millennium, proves itself to be God's authentic word by mediating God's presence, power and personal address to us in and by its record of men's knowledge of Him long ago. Still, as on the Emmaus road, nothing brings such balm and such a glow to the sad heart as to find that some part of Scripture, written centuries ago, nonetheless deals with precisely one's own personal problem, and that central to its resolution of that problem is the abiding reality of the person, place, work and grace of our Lord and Saviour Jesus Christ (cf. Lk. 24:13-35). Still, through the records of His earthly ministry, the quickening voice of Christ Himself is heard. Still, through the written word,

> He speaks, and, listening to his voice,
> New life the dead receive;
> The mournful, broken hearts rejoice,
> The humble poor believe.

Clearly, then, anyone who wants to know God will want to know as much as he or she can of what is in the Bible, and needs to know it too. Clearly, therefore, anyone who cannot read the Bible stands to forfeit a great deal of knowledge and of joy. Equally clearly, professed Christians who are able to dig into the Bible but neglect to do so cast doubt on their own sincerity; for inattention to Scripture is right out of character for a child of God.

Third: when I say that our attitude to the Bible (attention or inattention; compliance or defiance; acceptance or rejection) may determine our destiny, I have in mind the specific fact that all Scripture is a witness and a signpost pointing to the living, saving Lord Jesus Christ. 'You diligently study the Scriptures,' said Jesus to a group of learned Jewish theologians, 'because you think that by them you possess eternal life. These are the Scriptures that testify about me, yet *you refuse to come to me* to have life' (Jn. 5:39f.). 'God has given us eternal life,' declares John, 'and *this life is in his Son*' (1 Jn. 5:11). Paul congratulates Timothy because 'from infancy you have known the holy Scriptures, which are able to make you wise for salvation *through faith in Christ Jesus*' (2 Tim. 3:15). What Jesus and Paul say of the Old Testament may be said equally of the New, and so of the whole Bible: it all directs us to Christ. The written Word of the Lord leads us to the living Lord of the Word, and our attitude to Him is effectively our choice of destiny. For the one who truly attends to the Bible will attend to its God, and will learn from Him that the way to serve Him is to receive His Christ as Saviour and Master; and in thus finding Christ he will find life.

The contents page of the first printing of this book told its readers, 'R.S.V.P. denotes Revised Standard Version'. Not so, alas; but R.S.V.P. (*reply, please*) is precisely God's request to us in relation to Holy Scripture. I hope this book will help some to hear and meet God's request.

Two last points, both brief.

First, this is a study book, hence its compressed style (which saves paper, and thus, I hope, reduces the price to the reader). I have tried to ensure that clarity does not suffer through brevity. The Bible references in the text are neither ornament nor clutter, but part of my argument, and are meant to be looked up.

A VARIETY OF VERSIONS

Second, a word on translations. This century has brought forth a large litter of new versions, so many indeed that some folk now feel swamped, and by a natural if irrational reaction are resolved to trust none of them, but stick to the King James Version of 1611. In fact, however, all the main modern renderings are very good; no English-speaking generation was ever better served with vernacular Bibles than ours. They fan out. At one extreme are paraphrases and 'dynamic equivalent' versions, aiming at a total impact like that of the original on its own first readers. Such versions cut loose from the word-order and sentence-structure of the original, thus concealing the terms, and therefore the existence, of many problems of interpretation, and identify with one current literary culture. Thus, Kenneth Taylor's *Living Bible* reflects American 'pop' magazines and paperbacks, the *Good News Version* sticks as closely as it can to Basic English, and J. B. Phillips' *New Testament in Modern English* uses the full resources of twentieth-century English prose. At the other extreme are versions which as far as possible are word-for-word, clause-for-clause and sentence-for-sentence; the English Revised Version of 1881, and the New American Standard Version, go this way, but sacrifice smooth English in the process. Striking a balance between these extremes are two sober and steady versions, the New International and the Revised Standard, and two brilliant but uneven ones, the New English Bible and the Jerusalem Bible, a Roman Catholic translation. The two former aim at good plain English, and achieve it; the latter pair are more 'literary' in style, sometimes with odd results. All have the defects of their qualities and the limitations of their strengths.

So what to do? No perfect, definitive version of the Bible is possible, any more than a definitive performance of Beethoven's Ninth Symphony or C sharp minor quartet is possible; there is more in it waiting to be expressed than any one rendering can encompass. Both the word-for-word and the 'dynamic equivalent' versions are needed if we are fully to appreciate the meaning and force of the original: the former safeguards accuracy, the latter deepens understanding. I suggest that you try, as I do, to get the best of all worlds by having four Bibles at hand – the King James, with its majestic language and hallowed associations; a paraphrase; a word-for-word version; and one from the middle – and regularly comparing them. In any case, however, concentrate on one version for reading and memorizing. This brings most benefit with least confusion.

CHAPTER TWO

THE LOST WORD

'The days are coming,' declares the Sovereign LORD, *'when I will send a famine through the land – not a famine of food or a thirst for water, but a famine of hearing the words of the* LORD. *Men will stagger from sea to sea and wander from north to east, searching for the word of the* LORD, *but they will not find it'* (Amos 8:11f.).

Eight centuries before Christ, the northern kingdom of Israel was in confident mood. True, moral standards had crashed, little honesty was left in business, poor people were badly treated, and upper-class debauchery was a byword; but there was a trade boom on, money was flowing into the country, and society as a whole was affluent ('we never had it so good'). How could anyone be worried in such prosperity? Also, Israel had a national faith. Figures for church attendance were high. Public worship, with rich ritual and fine music, was a recognized part of community life (though congregations had publicly stated that they would not stand for sermons! – see Amos 2:12). Living on the capital of a great religious heritage, Israel did not doubt that God was on her side and would see her through all that the future might bring.

Into this complacent community God dropped a bombshell, in the shape of farmer Amos. Amos came storming into Samaria as a prophet of doom for Church and nation. God, he said, was about to judge His people (2:6-4:3). The wheel of retribution was already spinning, and would soon go faster. Recent disasters – the drought, the bad harvest, the famine, the epidemic, the earthquake – had shown God's displeasure clearly enough (4:6-11), and these were only a beginning; soon the whole nation would be enslaved and deported (5:27). (This happened fifty years later, under the Assyrians: see II Ki. 17.) Worse still, the streams of revelation were going to dry up. There would be 'a famine of hearing the words of the LORD'.

To appreciate what this meant, we must remember that Israel, as the covenant people of God, had been promised guidance by divine revelation whenever it was needed. Besides giving Israel His law, and charging the priests to teach it (Deut. 31:9ff.; cf. Neh. 8:1ff.; Hag. 2:11f.; Mal. 2:7f.), God had undertaken to send a succession of prophets, men with His Word in their mouths, who could give direction in times of personal and national perplexity. This was the immediate meaning of Moses' statement in Deut. 18:15, 'The LORD your God will raise up for you a prophet like me from among your own brothers' (cf. verse 18). In the passage from which these words come, Moses forbids the Israelites to take up with sorcery, spiritism, or any of the other occult practices to which the Canaanites turned for day-to-day guidance (verses 9ff.). To do so, he says, will be both ungodly and unnecessary, since God Himself through His messengers will supply all the guidance they need. Down the centuries, God had fulfilled this promise by giving Israel both great individual prophets who brought oracles for the whole nation (men like Amos himself) and also a host of lesser figures, 'seers' or cult-prophets, who gave oracles of guidance to individuals on consultation (for examples of this ministry, see I Sam. 9:6ff.; I Ki. 14:1ff., 22:5ff.; II Ki. 8:8ff.; and Num. 22-24). But now, Amos declared, God purposed as an act of judgment to bring this whole prophetic ministry to an end. Prophecy would fail (and perhaps the teaching of the law too: cf. Ezek. 7:26). Those who would not listen to prophets when God sent them (Amos 2:11f.) would find that there were now no prophets to listen to (cf. Mic. 3:5-7; Lam. 2:9; Ps. 74:9). However much people might desire a word of guidance or assurance from God, they would not be able to find one. Amos pictured the scene of spiritual destitution that would

result: restless, frantic souls wandering distractedly round
the country, listening to all that was being said in hope of
hearing God's voice, and listening in vain. Their hearts would
be hungry, and their hunger would go unsatisfied. For them,
the Word of God would be truly *lost*.

THE INFECTION OF UNCERTAINTY

Amos is a prophet for today. His words show us the present
state of much of Christendom. His vision of spiritual starv-
ation in Israel pictures ours: the famine with which he foresaw
that God would judge His people is the present experience of
a great part of the world Church.

Now this is an entirely unnatural state of affairs. The
New Testament represents the Church as inheriting through
Christ all God's promises of spiritual life and welfare (see
II Cor. 1:20; Rom. 15:8ff.; Gal. 3:16ff., 31; and cf. Rom.
4:16-23; Heb. 6:12-20, 10:15-23, 13:5f.). The Church, therefore, has the promise of constant instruction, assurance, and
guidance from God, just as Old Testament Israel had. Not,
indeed, that the Church is promised a perpetual succession
of prophets speaking by immediate inspiration, as in Old
Testament times; instead, the Holy Spirit, 'who spoke by
the prophets', is given to abide with the Church and to
interpret, authenticate, and apply Old Testament and apostolic teaching to each Christian generation (see Jn. 14:16,
16:7-14 with 6:45; I Cor. 2:4f. with verses 9-16; II Cor.
3:12-4:6; I Thess. 1:5, 2:13, 4:9; Heb 3:7ff.; I Jn. 2:20-27).
This is how the promise of divine instruction is to find
its fulfilment in the Christian era. In the light of this, we
would expect to find the Church of every age, including
our own, firmly convinced that the prophetic and apostolic
witness of the two Testaments is the Word of God; clear
as to its central message concerning God in Christ; and
able to see plainly how this message impinges on us, with
its demand for conversion and a life of faith, hope, love and
obedience. To the extent to which clarity on these matters is lacking, we are forced to conclude that the Church
is unhealthy and out of sorts.

What, then, must be said of the mass of our churches today? For at no time, perhaps, since the Reformation have Protestant Christians as a body been so unsure, tentative and confused as to what they should believe and do. Certainty about the great issues of Christian faith and conduct is lacking all along the line. The outside observer sees us as staggering on from gimmick to gimmick and stunt to stunt like so many drunks in a fog, not knowing at all where we are or which way we should be going. Preaching is hazy; heads are muddled; hearts fret; doubts drain our strength; uncertainty paralyses action. We know the Victorian shibboleth that to travel hopefully is better than to arrive, and it leaves us cold. Ecclesiastics of a certain type tell us that the wish to be certain is mere weakness of the flesh, a sign of spiritual immaturity, but we do not find ourselves able to believe them. We know in our bones that we were made for certainty, and we cannot be happy without it. Yet, unlike the first Christians who in three centuries won the Roman world, and those later Christians who pioneered the Reformation, and the Puritan awakening, and the Evangelical revival, and the great missionary movement of the last century, we lack certainty. Why is this? We blame the external pressures of modern secularism, but this is like Eve blaming the serpent. The real trouble is not in our circumstances, but in ourselves. The truth is that we have grieved the Spirit, and God has withheld the Spirit. We stand under divine judgment. For two generations and more our churches have suffered from a famine of hearing the words of the Lord. For us, too, the Word of God is in a real sense *lost*.

A WRONG TURNING IN BIBLICAL CRITICISM

Why is this? For it is not as if the Bible were no longer read and studied in the churches. It is read and studied a great deal; but the trouble is that we no longer know what to make of it. Mesmerized by the problems of rationalistic criticism, we can no longer hear the Bible as the Word of God. Liberal theology, in its pride, has long insisted that we are wiser than our fathers about the Bible, and must not read it as they did, but must base our approach to it on the 'assured results' of criticism, making due allowance for the human imperfections and errors of its authors. This insistence has a threefold effect. It produces a new papalism – the infallibility of the scholars, from whom we learn what the 'assured results' are. It raises a doubt about every single biblical passage, as to whether it truly embodies revelation or not. And it destroys the reverent, receptive, self-distrusting attitude of approach to the Bible, without which it cannot be known to be 'God's Word written' (Article XX). The result? The spiritual famine of which Amos spoke. God judges our pride by leaving us to the barrenness, hunger, and discontent which flow from our self-induced inability to hear His Word.

The situation is as paradoxical as it is pathetic, for critical scholarship has always claimed that its microscopic historical analysis of the books of Scripture gives the Church the Bible in a way in which the Church never had the Bible before, and in one sense this is perfectly true. Critical scholarship has sharpened the tools of biblical exposition and clarified the meaning of many biblical passages. It has given us commentaries of the highest value. It has invented a technique of analysing Scripture thematically without which the theological dictionaries and biblical theologies of the past sixty years could never have been written. In these respects it has paid rich dividends. It would be a sin against light to deny this. The 1958 Lambeth Conference was right to record 'our debt to the host of devoted scholars who . . . have enriched and deepened our understanding of the Bible'.[1] Yet the constant complaint against critical scholarship from its inception has been that it takes away the Bible from the faithful – the opposite of what it intends. And this complaint is true also. Here lies the paradox of the critical movement: that it has given the Church the Bible in a way that has deprived the Church of the Bible, and led to a famine of hearing the words of the Lord.

What went wrong, we ask, to produce such an effect? Why, this. From the start, biblical criticism drove a wedge between revelation (the Word of God) and the Bible (man's written witness to the Word of God). It viewed the Bible as a library of human documents, fallible and often fallacious,

and defended this as the only 'scientific' view. While allowing
that the Word of God in history was the writers' theme,
and that their writings do in some fashion mediate that
Word, it refused to identify the writings with the Word.
God's Word was one thing, Holy Scripture was another.
By taking this line, the critical movement broke with the
historic Christian understanding of the nature of Scripture,
crystallized by Augustine when he put into God's mouth the
words: 'Indeed, O man, what My Scripture says, I say.'[2]
Treating this view, not as a mystery of the faith, but as a
mere ignorant mistake, critical scholarship committed itself
to a method of study which assumed that Scripture might
err anywhere. It told the Church that the Bible could never
be rightly understood till belief in its inerrancy was given
up. It prescribed a new agenda for theology – not just to
integrate and apply the biblical account of things, but also
to check and correct it; and it condemned as unscientific
all types of theology that did not accept this programme.
Even today, its spokesmen remain convinced that those who
hold the Bible to be inerrant cannot really understand it, and
they still wage war against the classical Christian view of
inspiration. Thus, by insisting that the Scriptures are not a
fully trustworthy word from God, biblical criticism has taken
from the Church the Bible that once it had.

It is as well to say at once where, at bottom, this approach seems to go astray. Its mistake is to ignore the fact
that Jesus and His apostles taught a definite doctrine of
the nature of Scripture, a doctrine just as integral to their
message as were their beliefs about the character of God.
This doctrine appears in such statements as 'the Scripture
cannot be broken' (Jn. 10:35); 'it is easier for heaven and
earth to disappear than for the least stroke of a pen to drop
out of the Law' (Lk. 16:17); 'all Scripture is God-breathed'
(II Tim. 3:16); and it appears also in the designation of the
Old Testament as 'the very words of God' (Rom. 3:2; cf.
Acts 7:38). It is further manifested whenever Christ and His
apostles cite an Old Testament text to settle a point and
clinch an argument, or quote an Old Testament statement,
not ascribed to God in its context, as an utterance of God

spoken through human lips. Examples are, 'the Creator . . .
said . . .', Mt. 19:4, citing Gen. 2:24; 'Sovereign Lord . . .
You spoke by the Holy Spirit through the mouth of your
servant, our father David . . .', Acts 4:24, citing Ps. 2:1f.;
cf. Acts 1:16; 'the Holy Spirit spoke the truth . . . through
Isaiah . . .', Acts 28:25, citing Is. 6:9f.; 'about the Son he
(God) says . . .', Heb. 1:8ff., citing Pss. 45:6f., 102:25ff.; 'as
the Holy Spirit says . . .', Heb. 3:7, citing Ps. 95:7ff.; 'the
Holy Spirit also testifies to us . . .', Heb. 10:16f., citing Jer.
31:33. Indeed, this doctrine of Scripture underlies the whole
New Testament, gospels, Acts, epistles, and Revelation alike,
inasmuch as they all represent the Christian dispensation of
grace through Christ as God's fulfilment of His predictions
made in the Old Testament. The conception of Scripture as a
transcript of divine speech is just as basic to (say) the epistles
to the Romans and the Hebrews as belief in divine providence
is to the narrative of Acts, or belief in the Church's real union
with Christ is to the argument of Ephesians. Belief that (to
echo Augustine) God says what the Scriptures say is in truth
the foundation-stone of all New Testament theology.

That being so, the issue between the modern critical movement and the older approach reduces to this: are the New
Testament writers trustworthy teachers? and was the Lord
Jesus Christ a trustworthy teacher? What grounds are there
for accepting the New Testament account of any act of God
in this world, if we reject its account of His act of inspiring
the Bible? If, on dominical and apostolic authority, we believe
that God made His Son man, and redeemed us through the
Cross, and regenerates believers by uniting them to the risen
Christ, how can we withhold belief when the same authorities
tell us that God so inspired the biblical writers that their word
is also His Word? The grounds for accepting the instruction
of Christ and His apostles on this point are the same as they
are for accepting it on any other. The very reasons which we
have for believing what they teach about sin, salvation, and the
Church, forbid us to disbelieve what they teach about
the Bible. Certainly, the fact of biblical inspiration cannot
be verified by independent inquiry, but then neither can such
facts as forgiveness or adoption. We believe in these things,

not because we can prove them 'scientifically', but because we are assured of them by Christ and His apostles, whom we regard as teachers worthy of our trust. But we must not pursue these thoughts at present.

NEW VIEWS OF REVELATION AND INSPIRATION

A further fact heightens the paradox of our present situation. The era of biblical criticism has been marked, not only by intense study of the biblical text, but also by an unprecedented interest in the subjects of revelation and inspiration. Never in Christian history have these themes received so much concentrated attention as in the past hundred years. Never has the relevant biblical material been examined so thoroughly. And yet, for all this, the Word of God has been lost. Again we ask, what has gone wrong? Why has all this elaborate discussion, intended as it was to make the Word of God more plain and accessible to us, actually had a contrary effect? The answer is as before. The weakness of these theological discussions, as of the biblical studies that went with them, was that they drove a wedge between the living God in His revelation and the written word of the Bible.

Up to the nineteenth century, Protestant theology was accustomed to bracket revelation and inspiration together, subsuming the former under the latter. Revelation in the passive sense, meaning 'that which is revealed', was equated with the teaching of Holy Scripture, and God's revelatory action was discussed almost entirely in connection with the inspiring of the Bible. Revelation, it was said, was the process whereby God disclosed to chosen men things otherwise unknowable (a definition based on Dan. 2:22, 28ff., 47, 10:1; I Cor. 2:9f.; Eph. 3:4f.; Rev. 1:1f), and inspiration was the correlative process whereby He kept them from error when communicating, *viva voce* or in writing, that which He had shown them. A typical statement of this position is given by Charles Hodge in his *Systematic Theology* (1873). Referring to I Cor. 2:7-13 ('a wisdom that has been hidden . . . none . . . of this age understood it . . . but God has revealed it to us by his Spirit . . . we speak . . . in words . . . taught by the

Spirit'), Hodge writes: 'There is neither in the Bible nor in
the writings of men, a simpler or clearer statement of the
doctrines of revelation and inspiration. Revelation is the act
of communicating divine knowledge by the Spirit to the mind.
Inspiration is the act of the same Spirit, controlling those who
make the truth known to others. The thoughts, the truths
made known, and the words in which they are recorded, are
declared to be equally from the Spirit. This, from first to last,
has been the doctrine of the Church . . .'[3]

In the discussions of revelation and inspiration that went
on under critical auspices, however, this neat correlation was
given up. Also, the centre of interest shifted. Instead of being a
mere preamble to the doctrine of inspiration, revelation now
became a subject for study in its own right. It was seen that
the biblical idea of revelation includes more than the older
theology dealt with under this head. Revelation means the
whole work of God making Himself known to men and
women; the theme embraces, on the one hand, all the words
and deeds of God in which the biblical writers recognized His
self-disclosure, and, on the other hand, all that is involved in
the encounter through which God brings successive generations to know Him through knowledge of the biblical facts.
The Bible is thus the link between the revelatory events of the
past and the knowledge of God in the present. Inspiration,
therefore, should be studied as a subsection of the doctrine of
revelation, rather than vice versa. Inspiration is one of a long
series of steps that God has taken to make Himself known to
us, and ought to be treated as such.

This enlarging of the idea of revelation, and the dovetailing
of inspiration into it, seems biblical and right. Less welcome,
however, is the shrinking of the concept of inspiration that has
accompanied it. The belief that denials of the detailed truth of
Scripture, made in the name of natural and historical science,
were unanswerable, and, in particular, that Wellhausen's
theory of pentateuchal origins, which dismissed much of the
first five books of the Bible as non-Mosaic and non-factual,
had to be accepted (as it still is in most text-books on the
Old Testament),[4] led to reduced accounts of inspiration.
According to these, inspiration was an enlightening of the

biblical authors which, while it gave them moral and spiritual insight, and made their work 'inspiring' (or, as some say, a vehicle of God's Word to their readers), did not guarantee theological or historical trustworthiness to all that they actually wrote. Such accounts of inspiration are now largely standard in Protestant circles.

Hence, unlike their predecessors, modern Protestant theologians regularly insist that revelation and Scripture are two distinct things, and that to think of Scripture as written revelation is more misleading than helpful. Towards the close of *The Idea of Revelation in Recent Thought* (1956), John Baillie wrote: 'Each of the recent writers whom we have cited has been concerned to warn us against any simple identification of the Christian revelation with the contents of the Bible, and each has been well aware that in this respect he was breaking with a long-standing tradition.'[5] Once the idea of inspiration is weakened in the way described, this break is inevitable: we cannot identify the misconceptions of men with the Word of God. But now come the questions: if the relation between Scripture and revelation is not one of identity, what is it? And how, in detail, are we to distil God's revelation from the total contents of the Bible? It is easy to say that Scripture 'inspires', and 'mediates the word of God', but what is the cash-value of such formulae when we have constantly to allow for undetectable possibilities of error on the part of each biblical author? These problems constitute a blank wall at which many present-day Protestants are staring. Much writing is addressed to them, but no agreed or even coherent solution has appeared so far; nor, perhaps, is one likely to. Meanwhile, uncertainty about the Bible pervades our churches, and we suffer from a famine of hearing the words of the Lord.

THE ENFEEBLING OF THE CHURCHES

The loss of the historic conviction that what Scripture says, God says, is the deepest root of what James D. Smart, in a telling book-title, called *The strange silence of the Bible in the Church*. It has weakened Protestant church life in this century in a number of ways.

Firstly, it has *undermined preaching*. The true idea of preaching is that the preacher should become a mouthpiece for his text, opening it up and applying it as a word from God to his hearers, talking only in order that the text may speak itself and be heard, making each point from his text in such a manner 'that the hearers may discern how God teacheth it from thence' (Westminster Directory, 1645). But where there is doubt as to whether the texts of Scripture are words of God, preaching in this sense is impossible. All one can do then is purvey from the pulpit either 'church teaching', or else one's own private opinions. It is no wonder that the great evangelical preaching tradition of past days has almost petered out, and that many today have lost confidence in preaching as a means of grace.

Secondly, loss of conviction about the divine truth of the Bible has *undercut teaching*. Clergy are not sure what to inculcate as Christian truth; layfolk doubt whether what is taught in the Bible is worth learning. A spirit of unconcern about doctrine is abroad, a feeling that, since on so many issues it is anyone's guess what is true, it cannot much matter whether one has an opinion about them or not. Some clergy have ceased to try to teach the faith; many loyal church folk would not dream of trying to learn it. No wonder that a steady trickle of Anglicans, seeking certainty, turn to the Church of Rome or the cults.

Thirdly, uncertainty as to whether Bible teaching is God's truth has *weakened faith*. St. Paul is insistent that religious devotion pleases God only so far as it expresses faith; otherwise it is mere unacceptable superstition (see Acts 17:22f., 30; Rom. 14:23). But faith, according to Paul, means the subjecting of mind and conscience to the Word of God, recognized as such (see Rom. 10:17; I Cor. 2:1-5; I Thess. 2:13). In the absence of certainty as to just what the Word of God is, superstition prevails, and instead of faith there is fog. Professed Christians, though earnest and sincere, then become like the Jews: 'zealous for God, but their zeal is not based on knowledge' (Rom. 10:2). Much devotion in churches today is hazy, anxious, and joyless, simply because people have not been taught, or do not dare, to slot their

faith into Holy Scripture and venture their lives upon its
'very great and precious promises' (II Pet. 1:4) as the
sure words of a faithful Creator. Doubts and uncertainties
about God and our standing with Him are poor companions
to live and die with; but many today are never out of their
company, because they know of no assurances from God on
which their faith may rest. No wonder that the tide of faith
ebbs, and that church people as a body are in low spirits,
suffering from apathy and lassitude.

Fourthly, perplexities about Holy Scripture have *discour-
aged lay Bible reading*. The idea has spread that the Bible is a
book full of pitfalls which only the learned can hope to avoid,
that you cannot in any case trust it all, even when you have
found out its meaning, and that it is really too hard a book for
ordinary Christians to study with profit. Here, at least (some
feel), the Reformers, with their insistence on the clarity of
Scripture, were wrong, and the Romanists right! Well-meant
popular books, rewriting the biblical message in the light of
'the assured results of criticism', deepen rather than dispel
this impression. 'It is perhaps a pity,' wrote D. E. Nineham
in 1963, 'that the proposed new Anglican catechism appears
to regard the private reading of the Bible as mandatory for
every literate member of the Church. Is that realistic . . .?'[6]
Many would echo Nineham's doubt. No wonder the Bible is
not much studied by the average churchgoer.

Fifthly, and saddest of all, scepticism about the Bible has
hidden Christ from view. We are told not to think of the
person whose fourfold portrait the gospels draw, and whose
many-sided mediation the epistles describe, as any more than
a product of fertile religious imagination. That the Jesus of
history, the 'real' Jesus, differed significantly from the Man
in the gospels we can now be sure, and what was once
taken as revealed truth in the epistles must now be read
as the man-made, culturally conditioned mythology of the
Christian mystery-cult, telling us only of some feelings which
early Christians had. So the New Testament Jesus is no longer
the Christ who is 'there' (to echo the late Francis Schaeffer's
phrase); the historical Jesus is inaccessible to us, and 'Christ'
exists only as a legendary and symbolic figure in Christian

minds, like Robin Hood or Puck. Thus shouts scepticism
today. In the acid-baths of sceptical scholarship, the Christ
of the Bible has been completely dissolved. No wonder, then,
that relatively few in our churches seem to know, let alone
to know that they know, Jesus Christ as their Saviour and
Lord.

We have grown so used to this state of affairs that we
tend to regard it as natural and normal. Sometimes, indeed,
we represent it as a state of virtue (as is man's way with
his weaknesses), censuring our predecessors for being too
definite and dogmatic, and complimenting ourselves on being
open-minded, flexible, and free from obscurantism. We must,
however, be careful here. It has been well said that if you open
your mind wide enough a great deal of rubbish will be tipped
into it. The flexibility of those who are 'tossed back and forth
by the waves, and blown here and there by every wind of
teaching' (Eph. 4:14), 'always learning but never able to
acknowledge the truth' (II Tim. 3:7) is not commended by
the apostle. Obscurantism – shutting one's eyes to God's facts
– is always of the devil, and it would certainly be sin if, in
the name of loyalty to Scripture, we closed our eyes to (not
theories, but) facts found by history and science[7]; but we
cannot regard ourselves as free from obscurantism if, out of
supposed deference to history and science, we decline to face
the fact that New Testament faith is marked by dogmatism
throughout, and that this dogmatism is rooted in the conviction that the words of the Old Testament writers, and of
Christ and His apostles, were words from God. Generally,
however, modern Protestant theology does not reckon with
this fact; hence it breathes a spirit very different from that
of the New Testament. Self-styled radicals tell us that to put
new life into us we need a wholly new theology, one that
sits looser to biblical modes of thought than any before,
in which our twentieth-century Christian consciousness may
find its full expression. But if what we have said is right,
our twentieth-century Christian consciousness is already far
astray, and the course proposed would only lead us deeper
into scepticism and spiritual barrenness. It is vain to push
on along the wrong road. It would be disastrous to pin our

hopes to ever more drastic applications of the false principle that theology is an exercise in religious self-expression. Many clergy and academics, with desperate ingenuity, are already developing 'radical' theologies of this kind, in hope of alleviating our spiritual destitution and evangelistic impotence. But the epitaph on such theologies would seem to have been spoken already by Amos: *'Men will stagger from sea to sea and wander from north to east, searching for the word of the* LORD, *but they will not find it.'* Our condition will never be eased till we humbly retrace our steps to the point where we first went wrong.

HISTORIC REFORMED TEACHING

It will help us to do this if we now take note of what some of the formularies of the Reformation period teach about the Bible. Their position as a whole contrasts strikingly with that of many Protestants today. I shall quote most fully from the Thirty-nine Articles, Homilies and Book of Common Prayer of the Church of England, partly because these are the standards which I know best, partly because the Homilies and Prayer Book show us principles about Scripture finding practical expression in worship and devotion, which is our special area of interest in this chapter. But the Lutheran and Reformed foundation-documents all point the same way; their solidarity with regard to Scripture is complete. Their teaching may for our purpose be summarized under three headings, as follows.

1. *The inspiration of Scripture as the Word of God.*

Our formularies are emphatic that the ultimate author of Scripture is God Himself. The Bible is 'God's Word written' (Article XX), 'the very pure Word of God' (Preface, Concerning the Service of the Church). God 'caused all holy Scriptures to be written for our learning' (collect for Advent II; cf. 'God, who hast written thy holy Word for our learning': Visitation of the Sick). The Scriptures as a body were 'written by the inspiration of the Holy Ghost' and are

thus 'the Word of the living God', 'his infallible Word' ('An
Information for them which take offence at certain places of
the Holy Scripture': *The Homilies*).[8]

As such, the Scriptures are words of truth and wisdom: if
we cannot see this, the fault is in us, the pupils, rather than
in them, the text-book. 'It cannot . . . but be truth which
proceedeth from the God of all truth; it cannot but be wisely
and prudently commanded, what almighty God hath devised,
how vainly soever, through want of grace, we miserable
wretches do imagine and judge of His most holy Word'
(op. cit., p. 378). The Scriptures are wholly self-consistent,
for the God of truth cannot contradict Himself; therefore 'it
is not lawful for the Church to . . . so expound one place
of Scripture, that it be repugnant to another' (Article XX).
All that Scripture says, our formularies tell us, God Himself
says. Biblical teaching is wholly divine. 'We are taught *by thy
holy Word*, that the hearts of Kings are in thy rule' (Holy
Communion; see Prov. 21:1). God is the One 'who *by thy
holy Apostle* hast taught us to make prayers . . . for all men'
(Holy Communion; see I Tim. 2:1). From reading 'God's
cursing against impenitent sinners' in Deuteronomy 27 we
are 'admonished of the great indignation of God' towards
such, and so moved to repentance (A Commination). The
precepts and commands of Scripture are treated throughout
our formularies as abidingly valid expressions of God's will.
So are its promises: note, as one example, the words from the
prayer of St. Chrysostom, 'who . . . *dost promise* [the tense
is a continuous present] that when two or three are gathered
together in thy Name thou wilt grant their requests' (cf. Mt.
18:19f.). The gracious words which Scripture records Christ
as having spoken when on earth are words which He speaks
still: 'Hear what comfortable words our Saviour Christ (not
said, but) *saith* . . .' (Holy Communion; compare 'our Saviour
Christ *saith*' at the start of the baptismal services).

Also, the biblical accounts of God's acts in mercy and
judgment are uniformly treated as reliable, both as statements
of fact and as disclosures of the character of Him with whom
we have to do, so that we have prayers like this: 'O Almighty
God, who in thy wrath didst send a plague upon thine own

people in the wilderness . . . and also, in the time of King David, didst slay with the plague of pestilence threescore and ten thousand, and yet remembering thy mercy didst save the rest: Have pity upon us . . . that like as thou didst then accept of an atonement, and didst command the destroying Angel to cease from punishing, so it may now please thee to withdraw from us this plague . . . through Jesus Christ our Lord' (prayer for times of plague; cf. the prayer for fair weather, the second prayer for times of dearth, and the references to the Flood and the Exodus in the first prayer of the public baptismal services, and to Adam and Eve, Isaac and Rebekah, and Abraham and Sarah, in the marriage service).

A similar stress on the divine origin of Scripture as the authoritative word which God spoke and speaks is found in the Scots Confession of 1560, which speaks of 'the written Word of God, that is, the Old and New Testaments, in those books which were originally reckoned canonical', and of 'the Spirit of God by whom the Scriptures were written' (XVIII), and affirms that in listening to the instruction of Scripture the Church 'hears . . . the voice of her own Spouse and Pastor' (XIX). The First Helvetic Confession (1536) says: 'The holy, divine, biblical Scripture, which is the Word of God inspired by the Holy Spirit and delivered to the world by the prophets and apostles . . . alone deals with everything that serves the true knowledge, love and honour of God, along with true piety and the achieving of a godly, honest and blessed life' (I). The Second (1566) declares that 'the canonical Scriptures of the holy prophets and apostles of both Testaments are the true Word of God', having intrinsic authority; 'for God Himself spake to the fathers, prophets, apostles and still speaks to us through the Holy Scriptures' (I).

The ideas of biblical inspiration and authority which these statements reflect were amplified in the Westminster Confession of 1647. 'It pleased the Lord, at sundry times, and in divers manners, to reveal Himself, and to declare that His will unto His Church; and afterwards, for the better preserving and propagating of the truth . . . to commit the same wholly unto writing . . . The authority of the Holy Scripture, for which it ought to be believed and obeyed, dependeth . . . wholly upon God (who is truth itself), the author thereof; and therefore it is to be received, because it is the Word of God' (I, i, iv).

Since God is their 'only author' ('A Fruitful Exhortation to the Reading and Knowledge of Holy Scripture': *The Homilies*, p. 10), reverence for the Scriptures is a mark of godliness, while lack of reverent attention to them ('contempt of thy Word and Commandment': The Litany, cf. the third Good Friday collect) is the height of irreligion, and brings its own judgment. 'Be ye not scorners of God's most holy Word; provoke him not to pour out his wrath now upon you . . . Be not wilful murderers of your own souls' (*The Homilies*, p. 380).

2. *The authority of Scripture as a rule of faith and life.*

Anglican formularies define this principle of biblical control both positively and negatively, insisting that the way to serve God is by receiving and following all that the Bible teaches, without either addition or subtraction. They represent the service of God, in both liturgy and life, as a matter of observing what 'the holy Scripture doth say' (marriage service) and doing throughout what 'the Scripture moveth us' (Morning and Evening Prayer) to do, obeying the biblical commands, trusting the biblical promises and cleaving to the recorded doctrine of the apostles (cf. collects of the days of St. John the Evangelist, St. Mark, St. Bartholomew, St. Luke, St. Simon and St. Jude). The baptism services interpret the baptismal vow as a promise that one will 'constantly believe God's holy Word, and obediently keep his commandments'. The supreme good which we request in the Litany is 'increase of grace, to hear meekly thy Word, and to receive it with pure affection, and to bring forth the fruits of the Spirit', 'the grace of thy Holy Spirit, to amend our lives according to thy holy Word'. (Compare the similar request, that 'with meek heart and due reverence' we may 'hear and receive thy holy Word', in the holy communion service.) The supreme blessing sought for the newly-weds in the marriage service is that their life together may be ruled by the Bible – 'that whatsoever in thy holy Word they shall profitably learn, they may in deed fulfil the same'. The ideal for all Christian people is to 'desire God's holy Scriptures; love them; embrace them; so as at length we may be transformed and changed into them' (*The Homilies*, p. 371), in the sense that we may come to 'love the thing which thou commandest, and desire that which thou dost promise' (collect for Easter IV). The Scriptures are thus acknowledged to be, so to speak, God's mould for shaping our whole lives.

A formal statement of the supremacy of Scripture as a rule of faith and life appears in the opening sentences of the Lutheran Formula of Concord (1580): 'We believe, confess and teach that the sole rule and standard by which all dogmas and all teachers must be assessed and judged is nothing other than the prophetic and apostolic writings of the Old and New Testaments, as it is written: *Thy word is a lamp to my feet, and a light to my paths.*' This principle is in fact implicit, if not explicit, in all Reformation confessional statements; it is the great methodological axiom which gives Reformation theology, Lutheran and Reformed, Swiss, French, German, Italian, English, Scottish, Spanish and Scandinavian, its impressive unity of substance.

The Anglican Articles develop the principle of biblical authority polemically. Against Rome they affirm the sufficiency of Scripture. 'Holy Scripture containeth all things necessary to salvation; so that whatsoever is not read therein, nor may be proved thereby, is not ... an article of the Faith, or ... necessary to salvation' (Article VI). The first homily draws the moral: 'Let us diligently search for the well of life in the books of the New and Old Testament, and not run to the stinking puddles of men's traditions ... for our justification and salvation' (*The Homilies*, p. 2). Article XX states, also against Rome, the further principle that the Church must subordinate itself to Scripture in all its enactments. 'Although the Church be a witness and a keeper of holy Writ, yet, as it ought not to decree anything against the same, so besides the same ought it not to enforce anything to be believed for necessity of salvation.' All that the Church puts forward must be exposed to the critical judgment of Holy Scripture. The historic creeds are commended, because they pass this test

(Article VIII); but not all the recorded decisions of general councils and particular churches do (Articles, XXI, XIX); nor do such notions as works of supererogation (Article XIV), purgatory, indulgences, image- and relic-worship, invoking the saints (Article XXII), worship in a foreign tongue (Article XXIV), and transubstantiation (Article XXVIII).

The Articles also apply the principle of biblical authority to ideas attributed to Anabaptist sects, whose way it was to put too much trust in 'spiritual' insights taught by their leaders and to take neither the unity nor the decisiveness of Scripture quite seriously. On grounds drawn from the Bible the Articles challenge notions of the incoherence of the two Testaments (Article VII), of post-baptismal perfection (Articles XV, XVI), of post-baptismal sin being unpardonable (Article XVI), of salvation by sincerity apart from Christ (Article XVIII), of pacifism being obligatory (Article XXXVII) and responsible oath-taking unlawful (Article XXXIX).

A key principle of the Reformation witness to biblical authority is that all private and traditional interpretations of Scripture must be scrutinized lest unwittingly they misrepresent the detailed instruction of Scripture by distorting its plain, natural sense, as determined from within by study of the language used in relation to overall biblical idiom and other biblical passages. 'The infallible rule of interpretation of Scripture is the Scripture itself' (Westminster Confession, I, ix). 'The holy, divine Scripture is to be interpreted in no other way than out of itself' (First Helvetic Confession, II). The Church may not 'so expound one place of Scripture, that it be repugnant to another' (Article XX).

3. Our dependence upon Scripture as a means of grace.

All our material under this heading will be drawn from the Anglican formularies, for they are extraordinarily full and forceful on the subject. They regularly represent the written Word – read, preached, heard, applied – as the main channel of life from God to mankind. 'The Scripture of God is the heavenly meat of our souls; . . . it is a light lantern to our feet; it is a sure, steadfast, and everlasting Instrument of salvation;

. . . it comforteth, maketh glad, cheereth, and cherisheth our conscience . . . The words of Holy Scripture be called, words of *everlasting life*; for they be God's instrument, ordained for the same purpose. They have power to turn, through God's promise . . . and being received in a faithful heart, they have ever an heavenly spiritual working in them' (*The Homilies*, p. 3). Christ Himself, 'promising to be present with His Church till the world's end, doth perform His promise . . . in this, that He speaketh presently [that is, here and now] unto us in the Holy Scriptures' (op. cit., p. 370f.). Thus we are 'called by thy holy Word' to faith in Christ (collect for St. Andrew's Day). Through the Word we are sanctified: when heard and 'grafted inwardly in our hearts', it will 'bring forth in us the fruit of good living' (holy communion). It is through 'comfort of the Scriptures' that God gives hard-pressed Christians hope (collect for Advent II), and bestows on the individual 'troubled in mind or in conscience' 'a right understanding of himself, and of thy threats and promises; that he may neither cast away his confidence in thee, nor place it anywhere but in thee' (Visitation of the Sick). In all these ways saving grace (that is, living and working faith) is mediated through the Scriptures. Therefore we pray for confirmation candidates that God will 'so lead them in the knowledge and obedience of thy Word, that in the end they may obtain everlasting life' (Order of Confirmation). And when deacons are made presbyters we ask that their preaching of the Word may be blessed to us – 'that we may have grace to hear and receive what they shall deliver out of thy most holy Word, or agreeable to the same, as the means of our salvation' (Ordering of Priests).

The formularies are concerned that the Word be *publicly read*: hence the Prayer Book lectionary, covering the Old Testament and Revelation once, and the rest of the New Testament twice, each year. Hence, too, the mass of Scripture woven into the set services. No form of worship in Christendom prescribes so much of the Bible for public use as does the Prayer Book.

The formularies are further concerned that the Word be *publicly preached*: hence the ordination charge to presbyters 'out of the same Scriptures to instruct the people', and 'to banish and drive away all erroneous and strange doctrines contrary to God's Word' (Ordering of Priests). Hence also the prayer in the Litany (and the very similar prayer in the holy communion service) that God will 'illuminate all Bishops, Priests, and Deacons, with true knowledge and understanding of thy Word; and that both by their preaching and living they may set it forth'. Hence, too, the question to candidates for the diaconate, 'Do you unfeignedly believe all the Canonical Scriptures?', and the charge to bishops, 'Think upon the things contained in this Book. Be diligent in them . . .' The Prayer Book reveals an overmastering desire that Anglican clergy should above all things be men and women of the Word.

Finally, the formularies are concerned that the Word be *privately studied*: not just by the clergy, but by all members of their congregations. 'Unto a Christian man, there can be nothing either more necessary or more profitable than the knowledge of Holy Scripture . . . as many as be desirous to enter into the right and perfect way unto God, must apply their minds to know Holy Scripture.' 'These books, therefore, ought to be much in our hands, in our eyes, in our ears, in our mouths, but most of all in our hearts.' 'There is nothing that so much strengtheneth our faith and trust in God, that so much keepeth up innocency and pureness of the heart, and also of outward godly life and conversation, as continual reading and recording [that is, recalling] of God's Word . . . on the other side, nothing more darkeneth Christ and the glory of God, nor bringeth in more blindness and all kinds of vices, than doth the ignorance of God's Word.' 'To be ignorant of the Scriptures is the cause of error . . . as St. Jerome saith, "Not to know the Scriptures is to be ignorant of Christ".' 'I say not nay, but a man may profit with only hearing; but he may much more prosper with both hearing and reading.' Therefore, 'let us night and day muse, and have meditation and contemplation in them. Let us ruminate and, as it were, chew the cud, that we may have the sweet juice, spiritual effect, marrow, honey, kernel, taste, comfort, and consolation of them . . . Let us pray to God, the only author of these heavenly studies, that we may speak, think, believe, live, and depart hence, according to the wholesome doctrine and verities of them. And, by that means, in this world we shall have God's defence, favour, and grace, with . . . peace and quietness of conscience; and . . . shall enjoy the endless bliss and glory of heaven' (*The Homilies*, pp. 1, 3, 4f., 372, 377, 379f.).

But is not the study of Scripture too bewildering and dangerous a business for laypeople to engage in profitably? The first homily is at pains to insist that it is not. God is faithful, and will not let the humble go astray. 'I shall shew you how you may read it [the Bible] without danger or error. Read it humbly with a meek and a lowly heart, to the intent you may glorify God, and not yourself, with the knowledge of it: and read it not without daily praying to God, that He would direct your reading to good effect; and take it upon you to expound it no further than you can plainly understand it' (p. 6f.). The self-distrustful, prayerful Bible student will find that the meaning of the Word soon grows plain, one text interpreting another, through the illumination of 'the Holy Ghost, who inspireth the true meaning unto them that with humility and diligence do search therefor' (p. 8, quoting Chrysostom). The Bible is thus a book for all to 'read, mark, learn, and inwardly digest' (collect for Advent II), for their soul's health and as the means of their salvation.

THE TASK BEFORE US

There is a great and painful contrast between this rapt extolling of the Bible as our true light and chief means of grace and the casual, blasé, patronizing, superior attitude towards the Bible which is all too common today. Whereas the Reformers revered it, awestruck at the mystery of its divinity, hearing Christ and meeting God in their reading of it, we rather set ourselves above it, acting as if we already knew its contents inside out, and were indeed in a position to fault it as being neither wholly safe nor wholly sound as a guide to the ways of God. Both the spirit and the sentiment of the clergyman who once in a national synod spoke of the Old Testament as containing 'spiritual junk' are

unhappily typical of our age. Naturally, coming to Scripture
in this frame of mind, we fail to gain a proper understanding
of what it is all about. One of the many divine qualities of the
Bible is this, that it does not yield its secrets to the irreverent
and censorious. Down the ages the accusing voices of our
Reformation formularies charge us to consider whence and
how far we have fallen. They make us realize that through
losing faith in the Bible we have also lost touch with God's
law and Gospel, His commandments and His promises, and
indeed with His Christ, who is the Christ of the Bible. (And
what, after all, are the 'new theology' and 'new morality' of
our day but exotic ways of advertising our ignorance of these
things?) Our formularies teach us that our defection from
the Bible is in truth a defection from the Gospel and from
Christ Himself, and that this defection has brought us under
judgment. The application which we have made of Amos
8:11f. is confirmed by the following passage from the homily
entitled 'A Sermon, how dangerous a thing it is to fall from
God':

'The displeasure of God towards us is commonly expressed
in the Scripture by these two things: by shewing His fearful
countenance upon us, and by turning His face or hiding it
from us ... by turning His face or hiding thereof is ...
signified ... that He clearly forsaketh us, and giveth us
over ... when He *withdraws from us His Word, the right
doctrine of Christ*, His gracious assistance and aid, which is
ever joined to His Word, and *leaveth us to our own wit*, our
own will and strength, He declareth then that He beginneth
to forsake us ...' (*The Homilies*, p. 81.)

The present state of our churches makes it hard to doubt
that God has begun to forsake us in these days, as a judgment
for our irreverent disregard of His written Word.

What are we to do? We cannot recall the Holy Spirit
and revive God's work among us by our own action: to
quicken us again is God's prerogative, and His alone. But
we can at least take out of the way the stumbling-stones
over which we have fallen. We can set ourselves to rethink
the doctrines of revelation and inspiration in a way that,
while not refusing the light which modern study has thrown

on the human aspects of the Scriptures, cultural, linguistic, historical, and so forth, will eliminate its scepticism about their divinity and eternal truth. No task, surely, is more urgent. And this is the task which we shall attempt, at any rate in outline, in the following pages.

CHAPTER THREE

GOD'S WORD SPOKEN (I)

Basic to the New Testament is the claim that Christianity is a revealed religion. The Greek word translated 'reveal' (*apokalypto*) means to unveil something that was previously hidden, or to bring into view something that before was out of sight. Christianity rests on an unveiling of the hidden Creator Himself; Christians enjoy 'the light of the knowledge of the glory of God in the face of Christ' (II Cor. 4:6). The process, whereby through His dealings with a single national family – Israel – God revealed Himself to men, reached its climax in the person, words, and works of Jesus of Nazareth, God's incarnate Son. So the Christian revelation-claim finds its final statement in the majestic opening words of the epistle to the Hebrews: 'In the past God spoke to our fore-fathers through the prophets at many times and in various ways, but in these last days he has spoken to us by his Son' (Heb. 1:1f.). Of this revelatory process the sixty-six books of the Bible are both the product and the proclamation. The first thirty-nine (the Old Testament) span well over a thousand years of revelation to Israel; the last twenty-seven (the New Testament) were written in the second half of the first century. All these last have to do with God's crowning revelation in Jesus, who was crucified 'under Pontius Pilate' and raised from the dead, at some date between A.D. 26 and 30.

The opening words of Hebrews present the work of rev-elation as a divine activity ('*God spoke*') which in form was verbal ('God *spoke*') and cumulative ('through the *prophets* . . . by his *Son*'). In this and the next chapter we shall seek to open up the theme of revelation by exploring the significance of these three facts.

Revelation is a divine activity: not, therefore, a human achievement. Revelation is not the same thing as discovery, or the dawning of insight, or the emerging of a bright idea. Revelation does not mean man finding God, but God finding man, God sharing His secrets with us, God showing us Himself. In revelation, God is the agent as well as the object. It is not just that men speak about God, or for God; God speaks for Himself, and talks to us in person. The New Testament message is that in Christ God has spoken a word for the world, a word to which all people in all ages are summoned to listen and to respond.

To show what this means, we must here discuss three questions.

THE CHARACTER OF GOD

The first question is: Who is this God who has spoken? What sort of being is He?

The question is important, partly because misbelief about God's nature involves false views of revelation, partly because, according to the record, this is the basic thing that God's revelatory action was meant to make clear. God Himself was the supreme object of revelation from the start.

What, according to Scripture, has He revealed Himself to be?

First, He has shown Himself to be a *personal* being, one who calls Himself 'I' and speaks to man as 'you'. When, before the Exodus, He spoke to Moses at the burning bush, He gave His name as 'I AM WHO I AM' (perhaps more correctly, 'I WILL BE WHAT I WILL BE': Ex. 3:14f., N.I.V. margin; cf. 6:2f.) – 'Yahweh' [Jehovah] for short. This name, like other God-given names (Abraham, Israel, Jesus, etc.), was a source of information about its bearer: it declared, on the one hand, God's transcendent personality, His freedom and purposefulness, and, on the other hand, His self-sufficiency and omnipotence. The name 'Yahweh' is a standing witness against any notion of God as a mere impersonal principle: it declares that back of everything stands, not an aimless force – blind fate, or chance – but an almighty Person with a mind and will of His own.

When God brought His work of revelation to its climax by sending into the world His Son and His Spirit, He thereby showed Himself to be tri-personal – three Persons in one God. The Trinity is at the heart of the Christian revelation. 'Father, Son, and Holy Spirit' is God's New Testament 'name' (see Mt. 28:19) – in Karl Barth's happy phrase, His 'Christian name', expressing a basic truth about Him which only Christians know.

Second, God has shown Himself a *moral* being, One supremely concerned about right and wrong, whose dealings with human beings must be understood in moral terms, since they are determined by moral considerations. When at Sinai Moses asked to see God's glory, God proclaimed before him the following exposition of His 'name': 'The LORD, the LORD (Yahweh), the compassionate and gracious God, slow to anger, abounding in love and faithfulness, maintaining love to thousands, and forgiving wickedness, rebellion and sin. Yet he does not leave the guilty unpunished; he punishes the children and their children for the sin of the fathers . . .' (Ex. 34:6f.). God is perfect, not only in power, but also in love and purity, a God 'of infinite power, wisdom, and goodness' (Article I), 'a Spirit, infinite, eternal and unchangeable, in His being, wisdom, power, holiness, justice, goodness, and truth' (Westminster Shorter Catechism, Answer 4). God's own exposition of His name rules out all thought of Him as capricious, inconstant, untrustworthy, or unloving.

The impression is still abroad, despite many years of refutation, that the two Testaments represent God differently, the Old depicting Him as fierce in retribution, the New portraying Him as too merciful and mild to condemn anyone. But this is not so. The goodness and severity of God stand side by side in both Testaments. In the Old, the Holy God is unspeakably gracious to His people, as the Psalms constantly declare (cf. Pss. 92, 104, 105:1ff, 106:1f., 107, 108, etc.); while the New enlarges our view, not only of the glory of God's mercy, but also – largely through Christ's own words (see Mt. 8:12,

10:28, 13:40ff., 25:41; Mk. 9:42-48; Lk. 13:1-5, 16:23-29,
etc.) – of the terrors of God's judgment. In its picture of God,
as in other things, 'the Old Testament is not contrary to the
New' (Article VII), and the New, so far from cancelling
the Old, merely endorses and amplifies it, thus fulfilling it.
The God of both Testaments is one.

Third, God has revealed Himself to be the *source, stay,
and end* of all creation, and of mankind in particular. 'For
from him and through him and to him are all things' (Rom.
11:36). Paul develops these foundation-truths of theism in his
sermon to the Athenian idolaters about the 'unknown God'
(Acts 17:22ff.). First, he speaks of God as our *source*, the
One who brought us into existence. 'The God who made
the world and everything in it' (verse 24) 'from one man . . .
made every nation of men, that they should inhabit the whole
earth' (verse 26). Then Paul speaks of God as our *stay*, the
One who 'gives all men life and breath and everything else', so
that 'in him we live and move and have our being' (verses 25,
28). We depend upon God every moment for our existence:
creatures only remain in being through the constant exercise
of His upholding power (cf. Heb. 1:3). He, God transcendent,
above and beyond and apart from His world, and entirely
independent of it (cf. Acts 17:24f.), is also God immanent,
in the world as the One who is over it, permeating and
upholding it as the One who orders its goings and controls
its course. Lastly, Paul speaks of God as our *end*. God made
men, he says, 'so that men would seek him' (verse 27). Man
exists for God, and godlessness is a denial of man's own
nature. Humanity is only perfected in those who know God.
'Man's chief end is to glorify God, and to enjoy him for ever'
(Westminster Shorter Catechism, Answer 1).

This God, Paul adds, 'is not far from each one of us' (verse
27). Though He is 'Lord of heaven and earth' (verse 24),
infinitely great, He is not remote. Just the opposite is true. The
God who made the world is always, inescapably, our environ-
ment. Omniscient, omnipresent, unsleeping, undistracted, He
is before and behind us, ever taking knowledge of us, whether
or not we acknowledge Him. 'I the LORD search the heart
and examine the mind . . .' (Jer. 17:10; cf. Ps. 139:1-5). We

cannot hide from Him, even if we would; we live, willy-nilly, under His eye; and when He speaks it is our wisdom, no less than our duty, to heed what He says.

In 1963 J. A. T. Robinson's *Honest to God* was heralded by an article in one of England's national newspapers entitled 'Our Image of God must Go'. It is worth pointing out, however, that this 'image' of God as personal, transcendent, immanent, holy, the source and goal of all things, is actually a *revealed description*. Any alternative 'image' of God, there-fore, is false and idolatrous. In revelation, God tells us what He is like, and it is not for us to amend His testimony, as if we knew Him better than He knows Himself!

Certainly, the writer to the Hebrews thinks of the God who has spoken as corresponding to the description given above. God, to him, is the living Lord of the Old Testament (3:12, 10:31), the maker and upholder of all things (1:2, 11:3); a personal Being who talks to us (1:1, 11:7f., 12:25, 13:5), whose word searches the heart (4:12), and who knows us through and through (4:13); a God who keeps His promises (6:13-18); a just Judge (10:30, 12:23, 13:4), and a consuming fire against the defiant and contemptuous, who spurn the law and the Gospel (2:1-3, 6:6-8, 10:26-31, 12:29); a loving Father to His own people (12:5f.); a King whose throne is a throne of grace (4:16), and who rewards all who seek Him in faith (11:6, cf. verse 16). This, and none other, the writer tells us, is the God 'To whom we must give account' (4:13).

THE PURPOSE OF GOD

Our second question is: Why has God spoken? He is self-sufficient, and does not need men's gifts or service (Acts 17:25); to what end, then, does He bother to speak to us?

The truly staggering answer which the Bible gives to this question is that God's purpose in revelation is to *make friends* with us. It was to this end that He created us rational beings, bearing His image, able to think and hear and speak and love; He wanted there to be genuine personal affection and friend-ship, two-sided, between Himself and us – a relation, not like that between a man and his dog, but like that of a father to his child, or a husband to his wife. Loving friendship between two persons has no ulterior motive; it is an end in itself. And this is God's end in revelation. He speaks to us simply to fulfil the purpose for which we were made; that is, to bring into being a relationship in which He is a friend to us, and we to Him, He finding His joy in giving us gifts and we finding ours in giving Him thanks.

That God made man to be His friend appears from the third chapter of Genesis, where we find God walking in the garden in the cool of the day, looking for Adam to join Him and share His company (Gen. 3:8). That, despite sin, God still wants human friends appears from Christ's statement that God seeks true worshippers (Jn. 4:23); for *worship*, the acknowledging of *worth*, is an activity of friendship at its highest (hence 'with my body I thee *worship*' in the marriage service). God wants men and women to know the joy of the love-relationship from which worship springs, and of the worship itself in which that relationship finds its happiest expression. The supreme example of such a relationship with God is that of Abraham, who worshipped God and trusted and obeyed His word even to the point of being willing to surrender his son for sacrifice – and Abraham, we are told, 'was called God's friend' (Jas. 2:23, alluding to Is. 41:8; cf. II Chr. 20:7). It is to make us His friends, as Abraham was, that God has spoken to us.

And if He was to succeed in making friends, it was absolutely necessary that He should speak to us; for the only way to make friends with a person is by talking to him and getting him to talk back to you. Friendship without conversation is a contradiction in terms. A man with whom I never speak will never be my friend. The thing is impossible.

Friendship is never fully enjoyed while the friends are out of each other's sight. Looks express affection better than mere words can, and the delight of a love-relationship can only be complete when we are looking into the beloved one's face. So, when someone we are fond of is away from us, we write, 'I'm longing to *see* you again.' The Bible looks on to a day when the relationship between God and His human friends will be made perfect in this way, a day when, in addition to

hearing His voice, they will see His face. 'Now we see but a
poor reflection as in a mirror; then we shall see *face to face*'
(I Cor. 13:12). Similarly, Scripture tells us that in the New
Jerusalem those whom Jesus called 'friends' when He was on
earth (see Jn. 15:13-15) 'will *see his face*' (Rev. 22:4). Thus,
dying Mr. Stand-fast, in Bunyan's *Pilgrim's Progress*, could
confidently declare: 'I am going now to see that Head that
was crowned with thorns, and that Face that was spit upon,
for me. I have formerly lived by hear-say, and faith, but now
I go where I shall live by sight, and shall be with him, in
whose company I delight myself.' And by this vision both
friendship and revelation will be perfected. But meanwhile
God's friendship with men and women begins and grows
through speech: His to us in revelation, and ours to Him in
prayer and praise. Though I cannot see God, He and I can yet
be personal friends, because in revelation He talks to me.

Some modern divines posit an antithesis between 'personal'
and 'propositional' revelation, arguing that if revelation were
propositional it would not be personal, and that since it is
personal (God revealing Himself) it cannot be propositional
(God talking about Himself). But this is absurd. Revelation
is certainly more than the giving of theological information,
but it is not and cannot be less. Personal friendship between
God and man grows just as human friendships do – namely,
through talking; and talking means making informative statements, and informative statements are propositions. To deny
that revelation is propositional in order to emphasize its
personal character is like trying to safeguard the truth that
cricket is played with a bat by denying that it is played with a
ball. The denial undercuts the assertion. To say that revelation
is non-propositional is actually to *depersonalize* it. As Dr.
F. I. Anderson says: 'To belittle propositions because they are
impersonal is to destroy human relations by despising their
normal medium. The bliss of being loved is different from the
words of love-making, but the "proposition", "I love you",
is a welcome, nay, indispensable means to the consummation
of love in actuality. But in modern theology we have a Lover-
God who makes no declarations!'[1] From which it appears that
modern theology, for all its claim to stress the personal

quality of God's revelation to us and our knowledge of Him, actually takes a sub-personal view of both. To maintain that we may know God without God actually speaking to us in words is really to deny that God is personal, or at any rate that knowing Him is a truly personal relationship.

The God of the Bible, however, is a God who talks to human beings constantly: in visions, dreams, and theophanies; through the prophets, through Christ, through the apostles, and through the written words of Holy Scripture. He talks of His past achievements in creation, judgment, and redemption; He talks of the plans He is currently executing, and of the climax to which He will bring history when the time is ripe; and He talks of human life, telling us what He thinks of the different ways in which men and women live it, what His own scale of values is, what He likes and what He hates. So, by being propositional, His self-revelation becomes truly personal. And by it God makes friends.

THE PLIGHT OF MAN

Our third question is: What is the state of those to whom God speaks? In what condition does His revelation find them?

The biblical answer is that it finds them ignorant of God. The inscription that Paul saw on the Athenian altar reveals humankind's natural state: our Maker is to us all 'an unknown God' (Acts 17:23). None of the philosophies that Athens had mothered could help here: 'the world through its wisdom *did not know him*' (I Cor. 1:21; cf. Gal. 4:8; I Thess. 4:5). No one knows God apart from revelation.

The subject of humanity's ignorance of God is complex. To clarify it, two points must be made in order, as follows.

In the first place, being *creatures*, we cannot know God unless He acts to make Himself known to us. For fifty years before the First World War it was fashionable among theologians to maintain a virtual identity between man's mind and God's, and to try to distil conceptions of the divine nature from our highest thoughts and ideals. It is good that these notions are now generally given up. For the God of the Bible is One whom we can neither see (Jn. 1:18; I Tim. 6:16), nor approach (I Tim. 6:16), nor search out (cf. Job 11:7, 23:3-9), and we would fool ourselves if we imagined that we could read His mind, learn His character, guess His motives, or predict His movements, by our own unaided brainwork. ' "For my thoughts are not your thoughts, neither are your ways my ways," declares the LORD. "As the heavens are higher than the earth, so are my ways higher than your ways and my thoughts than your thoughts"' (Is. 55:8f.). 'How unsearchable his judgments, and his paths beyond tracing out! Who has known the mind of the Lord?' (Rom. 11:33f.). Emil Brunner points the application in a vivid phrase. ' "Canst thou by searching find out God?" To man's proud "not yet" the Bible replies "not ever".'[2] In Scripture it is axiomatic that human thoughts about God which do not depend on revelation are worthless. We can know God only through receiving revelation; not otherwise.

But does not God in fact reveal Himself to everyone? How then is it that the world remains ignorant of Him? This brings us to our next point.

In the second place, being *sinful* creatures, we suppress and pervert such revelation from God as reaches us in the ordinary course of life. That God constantly discloses Himself to every one of us as Creator, Lawgiver, and Judge, through nature, providence and the workings of our own mind and conscience, is perfectly true. Awareness of oneself and of the world really does bring an inseparable intuition of the reality of God and His claims. This is usually called 'general' revelation in contrast with 'special' revelation, the historical process recorded in Scripture. The fullest account of general revelation which the Bible gives is in the first two chapters of Romans. There Paul analyses it as God disclosing His eternity, power, and divinity (Rom. 1:20; cf. Ps. 19:1), His kindness (Rom. 2:4; cf. Acts 14:16f.), His moral law (Rom. 2:12ff.), His claim on our worship and homage (1:21), and His condemnation of sin (1:32). As against those who hold that general revelation, and 'natural religion' based on it, can suffice for mankind without the Bible, we must observe that Paul's analysis shows up the insufficiency of general revelation. It shows us, first, that general revelation is inadequate as a basis for religion, for it yields nothing about God's purpose of friendship with man, nor does it fully disclose His will for human life. Even Adam in Eden needed direct divine speech, over and above general revelation, to make known to him all God's will (cf. Gen. 1:28f., 2:16f.). Second, Paul's analysis shows that general revelation is doubly inadequate to the needs of sinners, for it lacks redemptive content. It indicates that God punishes sin, but not that He pardons it. It shows forgiveness to be needed without showing it to be possible. It preaches the law without the Gospel. It can condemn, but not save. Any unbeliever who rightly understood it would be driven to despair. However clearly the content of general revelation was grasped, it would by itself provide no adequate basis for fellowship with God.

But in fact we do not find among non-Christians a clear grasp of the content of general revelation. To a greater or less degree, they 'hold down [suppress, N.I.V.; stifle, N.E.B.] the truth in unrighteousness' (Rom. 1:18, E.R.V.). This is because they are 'all under sin' (Rom. 3:9). Sin, the ruling force, according to Paul, in every Christless individual, is a principle of non-conformity to revelation, and its effects are mental as well as moral. Sin prompts, not only disobedience to God's law, but also denial of His truth. Paul's analysis of general revelation in Romans is part of a great indictment against a sinful world for wilfully darkening the light that general revelation gives. General revelation, he says, is inescapable: 'what may be known about God is plain to them [all mankind], because God has made it plain to them. For . . . God's invisible qualities . . . have been clearly seen, being understood from what has been made . . .' (Rom. 1:19f.). Therefore idolatry and immorality are in every case 'without excuse' (verse 20), for they are always sins against knowledge. The formula explaining their origin is always 'although they knew God, they neither glorified him as God nor gave thanks to him, but their thinking became futile and their foolish hearts were darkened . . . they became fools and . . . exchanged the truth of God for a lie' (verses 21-25). Again, in Rom. 2:12-15, Paul appeals to the everyday operations of conscience as showing that all men have received through general revelation some

knowledge of God's law. Paul knows that non-Christian consciences act defectively, and are often silent when they ought to
speak (cf. Eph. 4:19), but (he says) when they do speak – and
everyone's conscience, however depraved, speaks sometimes
– their method of acting (judging by a standard), the standards
to which they appeal, and the actual verdicts they pass,
show 'the requirements of the law are written on their
hearts' (verse 15). Thus their immoral 'new moralities',
and their actual wrongdoings, are without excuse also.

In all this, Paul's point is not that of Aquinas, that the existence of God is abstractly provable by argument from created
things, but the much more fundamental point that God's
existence and law are actually known to all people, even where
both are denied in theory and in practice. Light constantly
shines, however much we shut our eyes and protest that we
can see nothing. Thus the fact of general revelation proves all
people guilty for their irreligion and lawless living, since all
without exception – would they but admit it – know better.

In fact, some of the light that shines always gets through.
Flashes of true moral and theological insight come to every
non-Christian mind (hence Paul, preaching at Athens, could
appeal to the poet Aratus, Acts 17:28). But these are only
flashes; no more. Calvin compared the isolated insights of the
pagan philosophers to lightning flickering over the benighted.
'Seeing, they saw not. Their discernment was not such as
to direct them to the truth ... but resembled that of the
bewildered traveller who sees a lightning-flash glance far
and wide for a moment, and then vanish into the darkness
of the night, before he can advance a single step. So far is
such assistance from enabling him to find the right path.'[3]
Thus, despite the occasional truths about God and goodness
which general revelation has planted in his mind, Christless
man remains ignorant of God.

NON-CHRISTIAN RELIGIONS

These considerations throw light on the nature of non-
Christian religions. In these days, when Eastern faiths are
resurgent, and Christian missionary advance is slowing down,

it is often asked whether God is not in fact revealed and known outside Christianity. The question is important, for our whole attitude to missionary work will depend on our answer to it. Do people of other faiths know God? A popular view has been that all human beings share a basic sense of affinity with God ('the religious *a priori*', as Continentals call it), that the only ultimate difference between the world's religions lies in the degree of success with which they cherish and express this innate God-consciousness, and that what the Bible records is a process of religious evolution through which man's God-consciousness reached its supreme expression in the teaching of Jesus (understood, or rather misunderstood, as essentially a declaration that God is the Father of all humanity). On this view, Christianity is certainly the Rolls-Royce among religions, the best of its kind, but the same basic sense of oneness with God underlies them all, just as the same basic design is found in all cars.

This amounts to saying that all religions, Christianity included, rest entirely on general revelation, which tells us of a basic harmony between God and ourselves – an insight most luminously crystallized in the thought of God as Father. It follows that no one really needs any more knowledge of God than general revelation can give him. But Scripture disagrees. It contrasts Christianity with other faiths at just the point where this theory links them together. Non-biblical religions (it says) are certainly based on general revelation in one sense, but it is general revelation (and in the case of Judaism and Islam at least, special revelation too) *perverted* and at certain points *denied*. Four factors (at least) have conspired to produce them: general revelation, demonic deception (cf. I Cor. 10:20; II Cor. 4:4), the smothering and distorting action of the fallen human mind, and God's judicial giving up of men and women to the nightmare state of believing what they want to believe and forgetting what they want to forget (Rom. 1:21-23, 25, 28). Non-Christian faiths, therefore, though resulting in one sense from knowledge of God, are actually forms of ignorance of God: modern non-Christians, like the ancient Gentiles, 'do not know God' (I Thess. 4:5).

Also, Scripture assures us that apart from the Christian Gospel all thoughts of natural affinity and peace with God are delusive. Where found (and they are not in fact common in non-Christian types of religion) they spring, not from a true reading of general revelation, but from self-deceived wishful thinking. General revelation actually discloses the wrath of God against human sin (Rom. 1:18, 32). There is no true knowledge of peace with God outside Christ. In point of fact, the dominant impression which a study of the great non-Christian faiths gives is of an agonized hunger for peace and fellowship with God, a hunger which these religions can evidently deepen but equally evidently cannot satisfy. Not that they are all entirely wrong, or wholly degraded; isolated truths peep through their theology at many points, and the ascetic discipline of the best of them is deeply impressive as an achievement of the human spirit. But in no case is their overall view of God and of the God-man relationship a true one. In particular, though they have all gained from general revelation some form of belief in cosmic retribution for evil-doing, they none of them know any effective way of reconciliation with the God whom man has offended. They know something of the law, but nothing of the Gospel. They seek peace with God, but, lacking Christ, they cannot find it.

Let me underline that in saying this I am speaking generally and comprehensively about the religions, not about any individual exponents or adherents of them, and what I have tried to put into words is a divine verdict revealed in Scripture, not an expression of human censoriousness or cultural imperialism. Present-day religious education distinguishes the religious dimension of human life from adherence to any particular faith and urges that all faiths must be appreciated in their own terms, which is right; and those who live in multi-racial, multi-cultural, multi-faith situations, as most of us now do, having friends and colleagues of persuasions other than our own, will rightly wince at any seeming disrespect for what these latter hold sacred. There remain lurking in the West traditions of contempt for non-Christian religions and their followers, as well as of uncritical confidence that they are all climbing the same mountain and will meet at the top, but the former are as indefensible as the latter. There is also a habit of measuring and censuring non-Christian faiths by reference to features which their own best teachers see as abuses, which is in effect to take them at their worst rather than at their best; this, too, needs to be apologized for and renounced, for if we think it would be unfair for a Hindu to criticize Christianity by referring to the various brands of folk-religion, civil religion, conventional formalism and plain superstition that it has spawned or embraced down the centuries we must allow that it is no less unfair to judge Hinduism, Buddhism, Islam or any other faith in that way. The truth is that not only Christianity, but all the great religions are capable of both degenerating and being reformed and renewed in their own terms; so they are only rightly appreciated in the light of their own highest ideals for themselves and their own intra-mural self-criticism, which means that humble, respectful dialogue is always the proper technique of approach to them while a brash triumphalist critique never is. Even so, however, the Bible reveals non-Christian religion to be as we said, a poignant kind of tragedy in which salvation is sought where salvation is not to be found.[4]

PEOPLE IN DARKNESS

Christless men and women, then, all the world over, are ignorant of God with an ignorance that is to some extent wilful and therefore guilty. 'Since they did not think it worth while to retain the knowledge of God, he gave them over to a depraved mind, to do what ought not to be done' (Rom. 1:28) – that is the divine diagnosis of all non-Christian religion and irreligion, and all sub-Christian conduct in the world. Underlying all the observable factors conditioning our beliefs and actions, which the human sciences can and do study, is the act of man refusing to respond to God's light, and the act of God giving him up to intellectual and moral darkness. God in judgment allows recalcitrant man to believe and do what he *likes* – hence all the false faiths and immoralities, pre-Christian, anti-Christian, and post-Christian, which filled the world as Paul knew it, and which still fill it today. (Could there be any account of the state of our race, as we know it from our news-papers and our own experience, more shatteringly up-to-date than Rom. 1:23-32; Eph. 4:17-19; II Tim. 3:1-8?)

There is in Anglicanism a strong rationalistic and moral-istic tradition of thought, going back beyond last-century liberalism to the seventeenth- and eighteenth-century Lati-tudinarians ('Latitude-men'), and beyond this to the Platonism of the Renaissance. Its habit is to assume that all human beings naturally aspire towards God and goodness, to treat the moral and religious intuitions of educated people as ultimate cer-tainties, and to take seriously only those elements of biblical teaching that fit in with them. Naturally, those who stand in this tradition concentrate on ethics, soft-pedal the themes of sin and grace, and tend constantly to endorse in practice the allegedly Anabaptist doctrine of salvation by sincerity ('every man shall be saved by the Law or Sect which he professeth, so that he be diligent to frame his life according to that Law, and the light of Nature') – a doctrine which Article XVIII condemns, on the grounds that 'holy Scripture doth set out unto us only the Name of Jesus Christ, whereby men must be saved'. It is this tradition which has led to the taunt that Pelagianism – salvation by moral effort alone – is the Englishman's special heresy! Children of this tradition find it hard to believe that men and women without Christ are guiltily ignorant of God, perverse more or less in their thoughts of Him, self-idolizers even in their outward worship of Him, and strangers to His friendship. Yet so it is, and it is vitally important that we should face the fact, and admit that, wise and foolish, rich and poor, young and old, white and black, we are by nature all together in this same boat. Even though general revelation shines upon us constantly, we are people in the dark. Apart from special, saving revelation – the revelation that centres upon the Lord Jesus Christ – we do not and cannot know God.

REVELATION TO SINNERS

The nature of revelation as an act of God is now clear. Revelation is our personal Creator and Upholder addressing us in order to make friends with us. We do not find Him; rather, He finds us. He sees us as rebels against Him, with our minds blinded and our characters twisted by sin, actively dishonouring Him by stifling His truth and serving false gods. But His Word addressed to us in Christ, though it begins as bad news, with a disclosure to us of the judgment under which we stand, is essentially good news; for it is a word of pardon and peace, a message of reconciliation by the death of Jesus and of 'a way back to God from the dark paths of sin'.

From this it appears that our study of God's revelation should be controlled by a recognition of two basic truths. The first is that what we are dealing with is a work of grace to sinners, a work, that is, of free undeserved favour towards persons who have forfeited all claim to favour. The Word that God has spoken in His Son concerns a costly and unmerited salvation that God has provided on our behalf. To speak such a word of grace is itself an act of grace, and only those who see revelation as grace can understand it aright.

The second truth to recognize is that knowledge of special revelation can only be drawn from special revelation itself. Only in the light of revelation – God's light, shining into our darkness – can we sin blinded creatures see light on any spiritual matter. And if we cannot know the truth about God save by revelation, it is surely evident that we cannot know the truth about revelation save by revelation. This means, as we shall see, that the truth about revelation must be learned from the Bible, just as the truth about God's character must be learned from the Bible. We must not be surprised if we find the Bible contradicting our own ideas, nor must we hesitate to recognize that if we depart from the biblical account of revelation, we go wrong. Many Protestant writers today err here, accepting the witness of revelation to other truths yet sitting loose to its witness to itself. Notions such as that revelation took the form of a progress from faulty thoughts of God to more exact ones, or that it took place by divine deed and not by divine word, or that the divine inspiration of statements does not guarantee their truth, or that the scriptural record of revelation is not itself revelation, get copied from book to book without regard for the fact

that they contradict revelation's own account of itself. Even
'neo-orthodox' theologians, who rightly stress that revelation
is known to us only by its own light, and that the Bible is
integral to God's revelatory action, have distorted their
understanding of revelation by importing into it rationalistic,
non-biblical axioms, such as the allegedly non-propositional
character of personal revelation (Brunner) or the supposed
paradox that God speaks His infallible word to us through
fallacious words of men (Barth).[5] We must be on our guard
against such lapses. We only truly honour the God who has
spoken in His Son to us blind sinners by listening humbly,
teachably, and without interrupting, to what He has to say,
and by believing, on His authority, all that He is pleased to
tell us – about revelation, no less than any other subject.

CHAPTER FOUR

GOD'S WORD SPOKEN (II)

In the last chapter, we thought of God's *general* revelation of Himself as Creator, a revelation given to all people through their own self-awareness and knowledge of God's world (see Rom. 1:19f.), as well as of His *special* revelation of Himself as Saviour, the revelation which is made known to us in the Gospel (see Rom. 1:16f.). In this chapter, however, we deal only with the latter.

The second major truth which the opening words of Hebrews teach us, is that *revelation is a verbal activity.* 'God spoke.' This is not a metaphor for some non-verbal mode of communication; the verb is being used as literally as any human words about God can ever be. The writer means, quite simply, that God has communicated with man by means of significant utterances: statements, questions, and commands, spoken either in His own person or on His behalf by His own appointed messengers and instructors. The rest of the epistle makes this quite plain.

THE PROPHETS

The writer introduces God as 'having of old time, spoken unto the fathers in the prophets' (E.R.V.). Who and what were the prophets? The currently standard New Testament lexicon, that of Bauer-Arndt-Gingrich-Danker, defines the Greek word *prophetes* as 'proclaimer and interpreter of the divine revelation'. The older lexicon of Grimm-Thayer gives a fuller definition: 'one who, moved by the Spirit of God and hence his organ or spokesman, solemnly declares to men what

he has received by inspiration, especially future events, and
in particular such as relate to the cause and kingdom of God
and to human salvation.' These definitions are indisputably
correct. In the Hebrew Old Testament, there are three words
for prophet: *ro'eh* and *hozeh*, meaning one who sees (a 'seer'),
and *nabi* meaning one who calls (a 'crier', like the old English
town crier). These words together give us the biblical idea of a
prophet. We tend to think of prophets as essentially men who
tell the future, but in the Bible the thought of the prophet as
predicter is founded on something more basic, namely, the
thought of him as a man to whom God speaks and shows
things, who is then charged to go and tell others in God's
name the things he has seen and heard.

The nature of the prophetic vocation is crystallized in God's
words to Jeremiah: 'I appointed you as a prophet . . . you
must go to everyone I send you to and say whatever I command you . . . *I have put my words in your mouth*' (Jer. 1:5-9;
cf. Is. 6:8ff.; Ezek. 2; Amos 7:14f.). To put words in someone
else's mouth is to tell him exactly what to say (see II Sam.
14:3, 19). This was what God did with the prophets. As they
repeatedly tell us, 'the word of the Lord came' to them, telling
them what they must go and say to others in God's name.
Amos describes their position, as mediators of revelation, in
two consecutive verses (Amos 3:7f.). 'Surely the Sovereign
LORD does nothing, without revealing his plan to his servants
the prophets.' There is the prophet as seer and hearer, the recipient of revelation. Then Amos says: 'The lion has roared –
who will not fear? The Sovereign LORD has spoken – who can
but prophesy?' There is the prophet as speaker and messenger,
constrained to declare the 'secret' that God has shown him. Essentially, therefore, prophets were forthtellers of God's word,
human agents through whom He made His statements public
and relayed them to the people to whom they were addressed.
But because God's 'secret' often included His future plans, as
well as the meaning of His present actions, the forthtellers of
God's word often appeared as foretellers of things to come.
That is how the idea of prophets as predicters fits in.

The hallmark of Old Testament prophecy was the prefatory
formula: 'The Lord says.' This formula proclaimed the source

and authority of the prophets' messages: it told the world that the things they said were to be heard and received as God's words, His royal announcements, and not just pious productions of man. Commonly the prophets spoke in God's own person: the 'I' of their oracles is more often than not Yahweh Himself. The psychology of prophetic inspiration, in which auditory, visionary, intuitive, and reflective factors were all involved, is necessarily mysterious to us who do not share it. But both Testaments tell us that, however mysterious, prophetic inspiration was a recurring fact in Israel's history from Moses on, and that this inspiration had definite and characteristic effects. It was more than natural insight, more even than spiritual enlightenment; it was a unique process whereby the human messenger was drawn into such complete identification with the message God had given him to deliver that what he said could be, and indeed had to be, treated as wholly divine. Though the prophet's own powers of thought and craftsmanship were fully exercised in apprehending God's disclosures and, so to speak, preparing them for publication, whether orally or in writing, the resulting product was as uniformly and uncorruptedly 'the word of the Lord' as were the Ten Commandments which Moses received on Sinai, written, we are told, with the finger of God (Ex. 31:18, 32:15f.). The effect of inspiration was that the oracles of the prophets declared, not the prophets' own mind simply, but God's. Nothing that they said 'by the word of the Lord' (I Ki. 13:2, 20:35) might be dismissed in the way that 'all the arrogant' dismissed Jeremiah's oracle (Jer. 43:2), as being a mere human mistake. What the prophets said, God said; as Hebrews 1:1 put it, God spoke in and through them, or as II Pet. 1:21 expresses it, 'For prophecy never had its origin in the will of man, but men spoke from God as they were carried along [impelled, N.E.B.] by the Holy Spirit.'

No wonder then, that the New Testament always treats Old Testament prophecies as true and decisive expressions of God's mind, and finds the chief proof of the divine origin of Christianity in its fulfilment of the prophetic Scriptures (cf. Acts 2:16-36, 3:18ff., 10:43, 13:22ff., 17:2ff., etc.). No

wonder that Jesus took Old Testament prophecy as containing His Father's blueprint for His own Messianic ministry,
and taught that He had come, not to overthrow the prophets,
but to fulfil them (Mt. 5:17; cf. 26:53-56; Lk. 18:3ff., 22:37,
24:25ff., 44ff.; Jn. 13:18, 15:25, 17:12). No wonder that the
apostles at once fell into the habit of citing texts from the
prophets as utterances of God, or of the Holy Spirit (cf. Acts
1:16, 3:21, 4:24ff., 7:48ff., 13:22, 33-35, 47, 28:25ff.). No
wonder that the writer to the Hebrews twice specifies the
Holy Spirit as the speaker of particular prophetic messages
(3:7 and 10:15, citing Ps. 95:7-11; Jer. 31:33f.; cf. Acts 4:25,
28:25).

When our author tells us that in Old Testament times
God revealed Himself by speaking the words spoken by
the prophets (for that is what it comes to), it is important
to see the range of his reference. We are apt today to restrict
the term 'prophets' to the authors of the prophetic books
of the Old Testament, along with Samuel and his successors
in Israel's history. But we need to remember that to the
New Testament writers Moses the lawgiver and David and
his fellow-psalmists are also among the prophets. The New
Testament hails them all as foretellers of Christ (Lk. 24:44;
Jn. 5:47; Acts 2:25-31, 7:37). Moses, indeed, was regarded
throughout as the supreme prophet (see Deut. 34:10), and
the Mosaic body of teaching as the supreme and basic prophetic revelation. When Stephen says that Moses 'received
living words to pass on to us' (Acts 7:38), it is the law of
Moses that he has in mind; the law, seen from this standpoint, was entirely prophetic.

A further truth to notice here about the things God said
through His inspired messengers is that, once spoken, they
retained validity and authority for the future. They are to be
thought of, therefore, not merely as what God *said*, but as
what He *says*. Within the stated range of their application, His
promises and threats bind Him, and His commands bind men,
as long as the world stands. 'The word of the Lord stands
for ever' (I Pet. 1:25, citing Is. 40:8). 'Until heaven and
earth disappear, not the smallest letter, not the least stroke
of a pen, will by any means disappear from the Law until

everything is accomplished' (Mt. 5:18). Since God's character and plans do not change, it could hardly be otherwise. And as God stands for ever to what He has said, so men in every generation stand under it. The words of the Lord never lose their binding authority. We express our sense of the abiding force of the law of the land by using the present tense when quoting it: 'the law *says*'. In the same way, the writer to the Hebrews expressed his sense of the abiding authority of the words of Ps. 95:7-11 and Jer. 31:33f. by using the present tense when speaking of their divine origin: 'the Holy Spirit [not *said*, but] *says*' (3:7); 'the Holy Spirit also [not *testified*, but] *testifies* to us' (10:15).

Not, of course, that the New Testament writers regard all the Old Testament words of God as retaining their original application. They interpret them, not in terms of the old, preparatory, typical dispensation under which they were spoken, and to which in most cases they had immediate reference, but christologically – that is, they reapply them in terms of the new situation created by the fulfilling of prophecy in the life, death, resurrection, and reign of the Lord Jesus Christ. The way in which, as we saw, Hebrews interprets Ps. 95:7ff. and Jer. 31:33f. as testimony by the Holy Spirit to New Testament Christians is a case in point. Accordingly, the New Testament recognizes that some requirements of the Mosaic law were only meant for the old covenant epoch, and were never intended by God to bind Christians: the law of circumcision, for instance (cf. Acts 15 and Galatians), or the Levitical festal calendar (cf. Gal. 4:10; Col. 2:16 23), or the sacrificial cultus (cf. Heb. 7-10, 13:9-16). The coming of Christ superseded these typical ordinances, and the divine instruction which Christians are to draw from them concerns, not God's will for their own present action, but the truths concerning God, man, and Christ, which the observing of these ordinances was always intended to inculcate upon Israelite minds. Similarly, the detailed Old Testament legislation applying the moral law of the Decalogue to the realm of public justice was only ever meant for the era of the Israelite church-state, though its ideal of fair, respectful and generous dealing with others should operate always and everywhere.

It is in this sense – that is, as witnesses to abiding principles and obligations – that these sections of the Old Testament law abide in force. We must remember that in the biblical conception of law (Hebrew, *torah*, literally 'instruction') theological teaching and ethical enactment are organically united, so that amended or expanded expositions which confirm the original theological teaching (as did Jesus' expositions in Mt. 5:21-48) could not be held in any significant sense to 'destroy' the law (cf. Mt. 5:17).

THE OLD TESTAMENT

We have not yet done with the witness of the author of Hebrews to the verbal character of revelation. We must now observe that he regards, not only individual prophetic and legislative oracles, but the whole Old Testament, as verbal revelation from God. This appears from a fact which makes his letter unique in the New Testament – namely, that he bases his whole argument, from start to finish, on Old Testament passages; all of which he treats as prophetic in the sense explained, that is, as authoritative disclosures of God's mind, even though some of them (those in 1:6-12, 2:6ff., and 12:5f.) are not, in their original contexts, words spoken by God in His own person. Thus, in chapter 1, the deity and kingship of God's Son are set forth on the basis of an appeal in verses 5-13 to Ps. 2:7, II Sam. 7:14, Deut. 32:43 (a part of the text which was only known from the Septuagint version till the Hebrew original was found at Qumran), Pss. 45:6f., 102:25ff., 110:1. Chapter 2 speaks of the manhood of the King in the light of Ps. 8:4ff. (itself an echo of Gen. 1:28), which is cited in verses 6ff. In chapters 3 and 4, an expository application of Ps. 95:7-11 is made, to show the need for believing adherence to the Gospel. In chapters 5 and 7, the Melchizedek priesthood of Jesus is expounded from Ps. 110:4. Chapter 6 treats briefly (verses 12-19) of God's faithfulness to His promises, the point being made by appeal in verse 14 to God's promises to Abraham, recorded in Gen. 22:16. In chapters 8 and 10, the fulfilment of Jeremiah's new covenant prophecy (Jer. 31:31-34) is announced and explained. In chapter 9, the meaning of Christ's sacrifice is shown from the significance of God's directions, enjoined upon Moses in Ex. 25:40 (cited, Heb. 8:5), for the structure and service of the tabernacle. Chapter 10 invokes Deut. 32:35ff. and Hab. 2:3f. (verses 30, 27) to underline the danger of apostasy and the need for steadfastness. Chapter 11 ranges widely through Old Testament narratives of how God spoke to His servants, and how they responded, in order to make the point that faith is a practical embracing of God's promises and adhering to them against all odds. Chapter 12 deals with the place of chastisement in the Christian life, by generalizing from Prov. 3:11f., cited in verses 5f. Chapter 13 sets forth the basis of Christian contentment in God's promise to Joshua (Josh. 1:5), which is quoted in verse 5 and followed by Ps. 118:6 as expressing our proper response to it.

Clearly, to this writer (and the whole New Testament is with him) the sentences and sentiments of the Old Testament are so many units of divine instruction, true testimonies to God's will, works, and ways, proceeding, in the last analysis, from His own mouth. The epistle to the Hebrews thus impressively illustrates what it means to believe that 'all Scripture is God-breathed and [therefore] is useful for teaching, rebuking, correcting and training in righteousness' (II Tim. 3:16). The writer's position is that not only the words of the prophets, but the entire Old Testament, first to last, is 'God's Word written' – that is, verbal revelation.

REVELATION IN CHRIST

Then the writer tells us that God has now spoken 'by His Son'. Some today argue as if revelation in the person of Christ takes us beyond the realm of verbal revelation altogether. But our author does not think so; rather, he regards verbal revelation as of the essence of our Lord's own revelatory ministry. This appears from his reference in 2:3 to the 'great salvation' which 'was first *announced* by the Lord, [and] was confirmed to us by those who *heard* him'. Here he focuses our attention on the verbal instruction – the 'word' – which Jesus and His apostles gave men in the Father's name. In this, be it noted, our author was simply following in Jesus' own footsteps: for Jesus Himself regularly reduced the question of whether men perceived God's saving revelation in Him to the question of whether they received and responded to His instruction, as to divine truth. (On the divine origin of Jesus' 'word', see Jn. 3:14, 34, 7:16f., 8:26, 28, 38, 40, 43 with 47, 12:49f., 14:10, 24, 15:15, 17:8, 14, 18:37. On the implications of receiving or rejecting it, see Mt. 7:21-27; Lk. 6:46-49, 8:4-21, 11:28; Jn. 3:11, 8:31, 37, 43, 47, 12:48, 14:21-23, 15:7, 17:6-8, 18:37.) Also, the writer is chiming in with the claims of Paul; for Paul announced his Gospel as God's long-hidden 'mystery' (secret), now made known to Christ's 'apostles and prophets' by revelation (Eph. 3:3-5; Rom. 16:25ff., cf. Gal. 1:12; I Cor. 2:10-13), so that it was 'not . . . the word of men, but . . . actually . . . the word of God' (I Thess. 2:13). For himself, Paul's claim was that by virtue of his apostolic enduement with the Holy Spirit (cf. I Cor. 2:12f.) he spoke as Christ's mouth, just as the prophets had spoken as God's mouth. Thus his evangelical teaching really was God's pure truth (cf. Gal. 1:6ff.) and his injunctions really were 'the Lord's command' (I Cor. 14:37). (On the divine source and truth of the apostles' 'word', see also Jn. 14:26, 15:26f., 16:12-15, 17:20; and cf. Rev. 1:1-3, 19, 22:6-9, 18f.). This array of evidence compels us to recognize that revelation in Christ, however great an advance it marked on what had gone before, did not involve any breach of the principle that what God reveals is made known to men by means of verbal instruction from God Himself. True as it is that the incarnate Christ was not only God for man but also man for God and that in Him we not only hear God speaking but also watch God blessing and man obeying, and that this is richer revelation than words alone could ever give, yet the centrality of verbal revelation remains, and it is precisely to the divine words that the Gospel calls us to respond.

Accordingly, at the end of the letter to the Hebrews, having referred to the 'voice speaking words' which Israel heard at Sinai (12:19), the writer sums up his appeal thus: 'See to it that you do not refuse him who *speaks*. If they did not escape when they refused him who *warned* them on earth, how much less will we, if we turn away from him who *warns* us from heaven? At that time his voice shook the earth, but now he has *promised*, "Once more I will shake not only the earth, but also the heavens,"' (12:25f., citing Hag. 2:6). The italicized words make it clear beyond all shadow of doubt that to this writer (and, once more, he has the whole New Testament with him) the essence of the Christian revelation is verbal communication from God, conveyed through Christ and His apostles.

VERBAL REVELATION UNDER CRITICISM

We have now reached the first of the watersheds at which the streams divide in modern discussions of revelation. The cleavage comes over whether or not we think of revelation as the writer to the Hebrews does, as divine verbal communication, God using human language, spoken and written by His special messengers, to make His mind, and so Himself, known to mankind. Many today hold views of revelation in history and in experience which move them, not merely to reject this idea, but to attack it, as positively harmful. This being so, it is important to be clear on just what the apostolic position does and does not involve.

First, some negatives, made necessary by current misconceptions.

1. The idea of revelation as essentially verbal communication does not imply the concept of God as a celestial rabbi who does nothing but sit and talk. It does not, therefore, cut across the stress which mid-century theology rightly laid on the fact that the God of the Bible (and, of course, of Hebrews!) is a living, active Being, the Lord and Maker of history, who discloses Himself by means of mighty acts of redemption; and that the Bible itself is essentially a recital of His doings, an explanatory narrative of the great drama of the bringing in of His kingdom, and the saving of the world.[1] Belief that the mode of revelation is verbal is in no way inconsistent with recognizing that the subject-matter of revelation is the living God and His redeeming work, as the epistle to the Hebrews itself shows plainly enough.

2. Nor does this belief imply that the receiving of revelation is simply a matter of sitting down and learning biblical doctrines. It is ironical when holders of the Hebrews position are accused of intellectualizing and depersonalizing faith. No modern theologian could make the point that faith is not orthodoxy alone, but 'existential' trust in the living God, more forcibly than Hebrews 11 does. In fact, as we observed earlier, and as Hebrews 11 shows (verses 7, 8, 11, 13, etc.), such trust is only possible on the basis of verbal communications from God – divine commands and promises – recognized as such.

3. Nor does the belief that revelation is essentially verbal communication from heaven militate in any way against the New Testament identification of Jesus as Himself the Word of God (Jn. 1:1-14) who discloses the Father (Jn. 1:18, 14:9). To argue otherwise, as some do, is like arguing that, because 'Flying Scotsman' is the name of a locomotive, it cannot also be the name of a train.[2] 'Word' (*logos*) denotes the expression of mind in reasoning and speech. God's Son is called His 'Word' because in Him God's mind, character, and purposes find full expression. God's revelation is called His 'Word' because it is reasoned verbal discourse which has God as its subject and its source. The verbal 'Word' bears witness to the personal 'Word', and enables us to know the latter for what He is, which otherwise we could not do. There is no inconsistency here. It is noticeable that, though Hebrews begins by hailing God's Son as the perfect image of His Father (1:3), three times out of four the phrase 'Word of God' is used to denote, not Christ, but the divine message concerning Him (4:12, 6:5, 13:7). (For other uses of 'Word' in Hebrews for God's verbal communications to men, see 2:2, 4:2, 7:28, 12:19.)

But what the claim that revelation is essentially verbal does imply is that no historical event, as such, can make God known to anyone unless God Himself discloses its meaning and place in His plan. Providential happenings may serve to remind us, more or less vividly, that God is at work (cf. Acts 14:17), but their link, if any, with His saving purpose cannot be known until He Himself informs us of it. No event is self-interpreting at this level. The Exodus, for instance, was only one of many tribal migrations that history knows (cf. Amos 9:7); Calvary was only one of many Roman executions. Whoever could have guessed the unique saving significance of these events, had not God Himself spoken to tell us? All history is, in one sense, God's deed, but none of it reveals Him except in so far as He Himself talks to us about it. God's revelation is not through deeds without words (a dumb charade!) any more than it is through words without deeds; but it is through deeds which He speaks to interpret, or, putting it more biblically, through words which His deeds confirm and fulfil. The fact we must face is that if there is no verbal revelation, there is no revelation at all, not even in the life, death, and resurrection of Jesus of Nazareth.

A CURRENT ALTERNATIVE

This point is crucial for current debate, since the view of revelation which, following writers like William Temple and Leonard Hodgson,[3] many British theologians have held in one form or another, really depends on denying it. According to this view, God revealed Himself in history by illuminating chosen observers of significant events so that they perceived what the events meant, in terms of God's character and plan. The events thus gained revelatory status through the coincidence with them of divinely enlightened minds. But this enlightening, though it heightened the observers' intuitive and reflective capacities, and sharpened their moral and spiritual perceptions, was not in itself an infusing into their minds of truths from God. As Temple put it: 'There is no such thing as revealed truth. There are truths of revelation, that is to say propositions which express the results of correct thinking concerning revelation; but they are not themselves directly revealed.'[4]

Many find this view appealing because, while it purports to safeguard the reality of revelation in history, it does not oblige us to treat all the contents of Scripture as truths of revelation. Fallible men, however enlightened, may yet make factual and theological mistakes, and on this view we have no reason to regard biblical authors as exceptions to the rule. Thus this teaching comes to terms with the methods of conventional Protestant biblical criticism, which for over a century has worked on the basis of a deliberate rejection of the idea of inerrancy. Those who take Temple's approach are thereby set free to enthrone historical criticism as the basic technique of Christian theology; and it appears that the number of those who see the theologian's task as, first, to reconstruct biblical history ('what *really* happened') from the biblical narratives, and then, in the light of this reconstruction, to assess the adequacy of the interpretations of this history which the biblical writers propound, is now large.[5] But the approach itself is vulnerable on many grounds.

First, it effectively overthrows the whole biblical idea of knowing God, having fellowship with God, and being God's friend. It holds that God's way of making Himself known, both to the biblical writers and to ourselves, is not to address words to any of us, but simply to guide our minds into right thoughts about Him as we watch Him in action. But this cannot in principle yield *personal* knowledge of God at all. As a Gloucestershire boy, I knew all about Walter Hammond, and when I saw him in action I had enough insight into cricket to tell why he swung his bat the way he did.[6] But I was never a friend of his, for I never knew him personally; he never spoke to me. On the basis of the view under discussion, we should have to conclude that no one, in Bible times or since, has ever had personal acquaintance with God, and, further, that the biblical idea of communion and friendship with God within a covenant relationship, in which He is committed to me as my God by promise, is an unrealizable dream.

Second, this view overthrows the biblical idea of faith, which is essentially of honouring God by tenaciously trusting to what He has *said*. When Abraham, whom the New Testament hails as the man of faith *par excellence*, 'believed God, and it was credited to him as righteousness' (Rom. 4:3; Gal. 3:6, citing Gen. 15:6), the object of his faith was a specific promise. (See also Heb. 6:13ff., 11:8-13, 17.) Hebrews 11:33 says that the Old Testament heroes 'through faith . . . gained what was promised'; but if the teaching under discussion is the whole truth about revelation, there never were any promises for them to obtain, or us either.

Third, this view compels the conclusion that God never in fact addressed words to any prophet or apostle at any stage, so that all their recorded experiences of hearing His voice must be dismissed, as C. H. Dodd dismisses the divine words of commissioning which Jeremiah heard, as 'actual hallucinations'.[7] This implies that, whatever they, in their hallucinatory state, may have believed about the source of their messages, we should never take their 'the Lord says . . .' as really meaning more than: 'I feel quite certain that if God spoke He would say . . .' Accordingly we must understand their authority, not as that of God speaking through them directly, but rather of themselves as theological pundits and religious experts, sharing with us their own beliefs about One who, though active in other ways, is dumb, and never speaks for Himself. But all this is highly unbiblical.

Then, fourth, this view overlooks the fact that in the case of all events of importance in the history of salvation (not to speak of many others), God did not leave their significance to be perceived during or after their occurrence, but prefaced them, often at a very long range, by verbal predictions of what He was in due course going to do. This happened, we are told, in the case of the Exodus, the conquest of Canaan, the setting up of the kingdom, the exile, the return, the coming of Christ, the Cross and resurrection, the sending of the Spirit, the calling of the Gentiles – the list could be lengthened further. These are facts with which the theory under review cannot cope; it can only be saved, therefore, by wholesale denial that these predictions ever really took place. Thus the theory disallows the claim made in Isaiah 46:9f., 'I am God, and there is none like me; I make known the end from the beginning, from ancient times, what is still to come . . .' If Temple's theory stands, then not only is this claim not a revealed truth, it is not even a truth of revelation.

Fifth, if there are no revealed truths, then the theological statements made by the Lord Jesus Christ are not revealed truths; and what, in that case, are we to make of His solemn assertions, 'my teaching is not my own. It comes from him who sent me'; 'I . . . speak just what the Father has taught me'; 'the Father who sent me commanded me what to say and how to say it . . . whatever I say is just what the Father has told me to say'; 'I judge only as I hear'; 'I am telling you what I have seen in the Father's presence . . . the truth that I heard from God'; 'my words will never pass away' (Jn. 7:16, 8:28, 12:49f., 5:30, 8:38ff.; Mk. 13:31)? Did our Lord suffer from hallucinations? Did the Father, after all, never speak to His Son? A theory that fails to allow for even the possibility that the words of Jesus have the status of verbal revelation surely stands self-condemned.

Further objections might be brought, but it already seems plain that this theory is untenable, and so we forbear.

GOD REVEALED THROUGH HIS WORDS

It will be helpful to set alongside this unbiblical, indeed, anti-biblical, theory a recapitulation of the position that we ourselves are arguing.[8] This may be summed up as follows:

What is revelation? From one standpoint it is God's act, from another His gift. From both standpoints it is correlative to man's knowledge of God, as on the one hand an experience and on the other a possession. As God's act, revelation is the personal self-disclosure whereby He brings us actively and experimentally to know Him as our own God and Saviour. As God's gift, revelation is the knowledge about Himself which He gives us as a means to this end. Revelation as God's act takes place through the bestowing of revelation as God's gift; the first sense of the word thus comprehends the second. Accordingly, revelation in the narrower sense ought always to be studied in the setting of revelation in the broader sense.

How does God reveal what has to be revealed in order that we may know Him? By verbal communication from Himself. Without this, revelation in the full and saving sense cannot take place at all. For no public historical happening, as such (an exodus, a conquest, a captivity, a crucifixion, an empty tomb), can reveal God apart from an accompanying word from God to explain it, or a prior promise which it is seen to confirm or fulfil. Revelation in its basic form is thus of necessity propositional; God reveals Himself by telling us about Himself, and what He is doing in His world. The statement in Hebrews 1:1, that in Old Testament days God spoke 'in various ways', reminds us of the remarkable variety of means whereby, according to the record, God's communications were on occasion given: theophanies, angelic announcements, an audible voice from heaven (Ex. 19:9; Mt. 3:17; II Pet. 1:17), visions, dreams, signs, the sacred lot (Urim and Thummim: I Sam. 28:6), supernatural writing (Ex. 31:18, Dan. 5:5), inward locutions, and what from the outside looks rather like clairvoyance (cf. I Sam. 9:15-10:9), as well as the more organic type of inspiration, whereby the Spirit of God so controlled the reflective operations of people's minds as to lead them to a right judgment in all things. But in every case the disclosures introduced, or conveyed, or confirmed, by these means were propositional in substance and verbal in form.

Why does God reveal Himself to us? Because, as we saw, He who made us rational beings wants, in His love, to have us as His friends; and He addresses His words to us — statements, commands, promises — as a means of sharing His thoughts with us, and so of making that personal self-disclosure which friendship presupposes, and without which it cannot exist.

What is the content of God's revelation? This is determined primarily by our present plight as sinners. Though we have lapsed into ignorance of God and a godless way of life, God has not abandoned His purpose to have us as His friends; instead, He has resolved in His love to rescue us from sin and restore us to Himself. His plan for doing this was to make Himself known to us as our Redeemer and Re-creator, through the incarnation, death, resurrection and reign of His Son. The working out of this plan required a long series of preparatory events, starting with the promise to the woman's seed (Gen. 3:15) and spanning the whole of Old Testament history. Also, it required a mass of concurrent verbal instruction, predicting each item in the series before it came and applying its lessons in retrospect, so that at each stage people might understand the unfolding history of salvation, hope in the promise of its full accomplishment, and learn what manner of persons they, as objects of grace, ought to be. Thus the history of salvation (the acts of God) took place in the context of the history of revelation (the oracles of God).

But the epoch of revelation ended with Christ and the apostles: how, then, does God reveal Himself to us today? By saying to us the same thing that He said to others long ago, only now in direct application to ourselves, in the situation in which we are. The biblical idea, as we saw, is that God's words, spoken at particular moments in biblical history, have binding force for all succeeding generations. He does not change; and therefore His assertions, once made, remain true, to govern every individual's thinking. The judgments He once passed on particular individuals or groups stand for ever as a revelation of His character and of the standards by which He measures us all. Similarly, His moral instruction remains valid as declaring His ideals for all our lives. God's historical utterances thus operate like statute law in society. Enactments of various dates, once on the statute book, remain continually in force, applying in principle to everyone (though it may need hard thinking and careful arguing to show just how), and each generation is obliged to comply with what 'the law says'. In the same way, we are all under obligation to God, to do as His words, spoken at different times in biblical history, require – or, as we put it, to be ruled by what 'the word of God says'.

The utterances of God thus function (to change the illustration) like the words of a university tutor in a group tutorial, where one person brings and reads an essay and the rest of the group learns by hearing the tutor's comments on it. As the history of the words of God passes before us in our Bible reading and our hearing of sermons, it is as if we were in a group tutorial with Abraham, Moses, David, Elijah, Peter, the Israelites, the Christians of Rome, the Galatian believers, the seven churches of the Apocalypse, and all the rest of those to whom particular words of God were addressed, and with whom His dealings are recorded. We overhear what God is saying to them as He comments on what they have done and gives them advice and guidance for the future, and from this we learn what He would say to us about our own lives. And, just as the listener in a joint tutorial under a shrewd teacher who knows his pupils will often feel, and with reason, that the comments called forth by the essay have been 'angled' to give needed instruction to all present as well as to the essayist himself, so Christians studying the recorded words of God will often feel that what God said to someone thousands of years ago speaks to their own condition so perfectly that it might have been written specially for them. (And so, of course, it was! – for, just as all Christians can truly say, with Paul, that Christ 'loved me and gave himself for me' [Gal. 2:20], so they can truly say that God 'loved me, and wrote this book for me'. What God caused to be written for the Church in general [cf. I Cor. 10:11; Rom. 15:4] He caused to be written for each Christian individually. The devotional maxim that one should read the Scriptures as one would read a personal letter from one's best friend rests not on pious fancy, but on the hardest theological fact.)

This illustration is one-sided (aren't they all?); it could leave the impression that God only speaks to us to get our thoughts straight. So I add to it another, that of the trainer who coaches you in a sport. His job is to drill you into doing everything correctly – which means, among other things, better than hitherto. He is, therefore, a perfectionist, and he makes you vividly aware of that fact. He invades the privacy of your comfortable bad habits with intrusive words which sometimes make you smart. He watches all your movements, letting nothing pass, requiring you to do things differently in a way that at first seems awkward and chiding you, fiercely perhaps, when you go on in, or fall back into, the old ways. Sometimes he will act angry at you, and denounce you before others, or get them to watch and criticize you, in a way which your pride resents; sometimes he makes you hate his guts and wish he were not there. But in your sober moments you know it is in a good cause; he is committed to changing you for the better, and his very persistence in bawling you out for second-rate performance is really an affirmation of you, for unless he saw that you could improve he would not waste time and energy on you. Nobody was ever ruder and more savage with the musicians whom he rehearsed than the late Arturo Toscanini, but he trained orchestras to achieve a balance and precision of which they had never before dreamed, and most of those who experienced him said afterwards that there was no one under whom they would rather play. Here is a further picture of what God is doing to you and me through His words to us and His providential ordering of things. He reproves, corrects and instructs in righteousness; He is training us 'that we may share in his holiness. No discipline seems pleasant at the time, but painful. Later on, however, it produces a harvest of righteousness and peace for those who have been trained by it' (Heb. 12:10f.). This is what God is aiming at when He speaks afresh His words of long ago in application to our lives.

THE PROGRESS OF REVELATION

The final truth which the opening words of Hebrews teach is that *revelation is a cumulative activity*. God's revelation in Christ does not stand alone, but comes as the climax of a long series of revelatory disclosures. The statement that in Old Testament times God spoke (as the *New English Bible* puts it) 'in fragmentary and varied fashion through the prophets' covers the earlier items in the series. 'But in this the final age', the same version continues, 'he has spoken to us in the Son.'

'In fragmentary and varied fashion . . . in the Son . . .' Here is implied, not only a climax, but also a contrast between a revelation, or series of revelations, that was partial and incomplete, a thing of bits and pieces, not fully integrated, and a revelation that was comprehensive, unified, and final. How should we interpret this contrast? The rest of the epistle shows us. It is the contrast, not between crude and refined, 'primitive' and 'evolved', partly false and wholly true, but between promises and their fulfilment, types and the antitype, shadows and substance, incompleteness and perfection, in the two successive dispensations of divine grace under which God's covenant people have successively lived. It is a contrast to be expounded in terms, not of better conceptions of God, but of the better covenant (Heb. 7:22), the better priest (7:26ff.), the better sacrifice (9:23), the better promises (8:6), the better hope (7:19), the fuller access (9:8f., 10:19ff.), and the livelier foretastes of glory (6:4f.), that Christians have through Christ as compared with Old Testament believers; as also in terms of the fact that the Gospel of Christ is for Jew and Gentile alike, whereas the Old Testament revelation was addressed to Jews only (cf. Ps. 147:19f.). The phrase 'in fragmentary . . . fashion' denotes simply, as John Owen saw long ago, that 'the will of God concerning His worship and obedience, was not formerly revealed all at once to His Church, by Moses or any other', but that its revelation was a gradual process, 'by the addition of one thing after another, at several seasons, as the Church could bear the light of them, and as it was subserving to His main design of reserving all pre-eminence to the Messiah'.[9] Then, in New Testament times, just as all roads were said to lead to Rome, so all the diverse and seemingly divergent strands of Old Testament revelation were found to lead to Jesus Christ, prophet, priest, and king, mediator, sacrifice, and intercessor, crucified, risen, and coming again.

Since the New Testament represents in these ways an advance on the Old, may we not speak of revelation as progressive? It all depends on what we mean by 'progressive'. If our meaning is simply that God's Old Testament utterances, however diverse, all contributed in one way or another to His 'build-up' for the coming of His Son, the word is acceptable enough. But much liberal theology has used the word to express the idea that the history of revelation is really the history of how Israel's thoughts of God evolved from something very crude (a tribal war-god) through something more refined (a moral Creator) to the conception of God taught by Jesus (a loving Father); and has set forth this idea in such a way as to imply that Christians need not bother with the Old Testament at all, since all that is true in its view of God can be learned from the New Testament, and all the rest of what it says about Him is more or less false. But this is not so. God was certainly amplifying people's knowledge about Himself throughout the revelatory process, but the idea that what was revealed later contradicts and cancels what was revealed earlier is wrong. So is the widespread neglect of the Old Testament to which this idea has led. The New Testament revelation rests at every point on the Old as its foundation, and to remove the foundation once the superstructure is in place is the surest way to dislodge the superstructure itself. Those who neglect the Old Testament will never make much of the New. When, therefore, the phrase 'progressive revelation' is used as a label for this myth of evolutionary religious development, and hence as a justification for disregarding the Old Testament, it is false, and since the word 'progressive' has been pressed into service so often in this sense, it is best to eschew it – simply to avoid confusion – when stating the biblical position. The belief that later revelation, so far from conflicting with what had gone before, presupposed it and built on it at each stage, is best expressed by calling the revelatory process 'cumulative' rather than 'progressive'.

But if the progress of revelation in history over a thousand years and more was cumulative, and if the later items in the series of God's words built on those that had gone before, then it is clear that these later items can only be interpreted in the light of the series as a whole, and in particular that the last item of all – God's Word spoken by His Son – is further from being self-interpreting than any, and needs to be set in the context of all God's earlier words before it can be properly understood. Which means that the very nature of the revelatory process itself made it necessary that a unified record of God's words should be provided. Just as, if we sinners were ever to know God as our Friend, He had to speak to us about redemption, so, if the sequence of His words was to have its intended effect upon us, there had to be a total presentation of it in permanently accessible form – in other words, there had to be a Bible. Confirmation of this reasoning lies in the fact that God actually has given us just such a Bible – a book made up of many books, which grew to its present size in step with the ongoing revelatory process itself, and which now stands as a full explanatory narrative of the saving words and deeds of God. As Calvin put it, 'in order that, with the constant forward march of divine instruction (*continuo progressu doctrinae*), God's truth might remain a survivor in the world in all ages, He willed that the oracles which He had deposited with the fathers should be, so to speak, consigned to public records.'[10] So the Bible, a book thrown up by the revelatory process in history, was no accidental by-product of that process, but an integral and indispensable part of it; for without a record of God's earlier revelations, His later words and, most of all, His last Word, could not be fully understood. Nor, without a permanent record of the whole process, could God's revelation as a whole be preserved against corruption to do in each generation its own proper work of bringing sinners to know God.

So God's work of producing and preserving the books that make up the Bible should be celebrated as displaying not only His power, but His wisdom too; and any denial that we can fully trust the Bible for our knowledge of Christ and His salvation should be seen as, in effect, accusing God of real impotence, or real folly, or both.

CHAPTER FIVE

GOD'S WORD WRITTEN

In this chapter, we shall sketch in the view of Holy Scripture to which the last two chapters have been pointing – which is, in fact, in all essentials the view embodied in our historical Anglican formularies.[1] To clear our path, we start with some further comments on the 'critical' study of Scripture, as practised today.

THE 'CRITICAL' METHOD

What marks off the 'critical' movement, so-called, from the biblical scholarship of earlier days is that it approaches the Bible first and foremost as a book of ancient history, and studies it in the light of a view of history as a developing process with its own causal laws inherent in itself – a view which came of age as one of the secularized, 'scientific' speculations which filled the German universities in the last century. Accordingly, biblical study in Protestant centres of learning, as witness their textbooks and examination papers, is now dominated by, on the one hand, minute enquiry into the sources, dates, authorship, occasion, and purpose, of the various biblical books, and, on the other hand, attempts to reconstruct from the 'modern' point of view, as an intelligible self-contained process, the sequence of events which the Bible itself narrates as the story of God's work in creation, providence, and grace.

It is clear that this method, as described, squares more easily with a naturalistic, evolutionary, anti-miraculous, uniformitarian outlook than it does with any form of the belief that biblical and Church history, while conditioned at all points by prior factors which historians can tabulate, has actually been *caused* by repeated intrusions (revelatory, miraculous, regenerative) of the power of God in *new creation*, intrusions which produce in the lives of men and nations effects that are ultimately inexplicable in terms of what went before. And in fact the pioneers of historical biblical criticism linked their enterprise so closely to anti-supernatural axioms, including a dogmatic denial of biblical inerrancy, that an impression was created that biblical study would not be 'scientific' at all, in any sense, if done on any other basis. From this secular superstition – for such it is – later Protestant scholarship has never quite broken free. (Its Roman counterpart, which, though embracing the historical approach, cleaves to an explicit supernaturalism and an equally explicit doctrine of biblical inerrancy has on the whole done better at this point.[2]) Today, most English Protestant scholars, more conservative, as ever, than their opposite numbers in Germany and America, guardedly accept the miraculous and maintain, however blurrily, the broad outlines of the biblical faith; but almost to a man they still execrate the doctrine of inerrancy. Meanwhile, 'biblical criticism' remains identified in many Christian minds with an unlawful craving to tone down the Bible and justify unorthodox beliefs, and so continues suspect.

It needs to be said clearly that, though such distorting pseudo-scientific assumptions as those mentioned must certainly be rejected, the use of an historical method of studying Scripture is a theological necessity none the less. For God's revelation really did take the form of an historical process; God's Word concerning it really does take the form of a book of ancient history; the reality of biblical inspiration does imply that we learn God's message through finding out what the human writers meant (for what they said, He says); and unless we understand their statements historically – in terms, that is, of their intended meaning when first made – we are bound to misunderstand them, more or less. This was the point of the Reformers' insistence that Scripture must be interpreted 'literally', as opposed to allegorically. Their plea was for what in the American tongue is known as 'grammatico-historical' exegesis – a technique of which, by common consent, John Calvin himself was as great a master as the Church ever had. The truth is that, as Jesus of Nazareth was no less truly human than divine, so it is with the Scriptures. The mystery of the Word incarnate is at this point parallel to that of the Word written. And as we must see Jesus in His human, historical context, and study His recorded words as the sayings of a first-century Jew, if we would fully grasp their message to us as words of God, so it is in interpreting all the words of the Bible. Therefore enquiry into the linguistic, cultural, historical, and theological background of the various parts of Holy Scripture, and into the outlook and aims of their respective authors, must be welcomed as a necessary discipline if the Bible is to be rightly understood. Historical criticism, then, though in the past abused, is really essential; there can be no good commentaries, or accurate exposition, or sound theology, without it. We do well to remember at this point that the proper meaning of 'criticism' is not *censure*, as such, but *appreciation*. It would be as misguided to discourage appreciative study of the human aspects of Scripture, for fear of losing our grip on its divinity, as it would be to discourage frank recognition of the manhood of our Lord on similar grounds. The only proviso is that our study of the Bible, as of Christ Himself, must be based on fully biblical presuppositions about that which we are studying.

SOME INADEQUATE POSITIONS

Those who, following the current conventions of criticism, reject Augustine's axiom that what Scripture says, God says, divide sharply over the questions of how God's truth reaches us, and what its content is. Thus, for instance, Anglican 'broad churchmen' in the Platonist tradition, like the authors of *Essays and Reviews*, in the last century, still think of revelation in terms of a quickening of conscience to embrace moral and spiritual imperatives on the basis of a robust cosmic optimism – a belief, that is, that goodness will triumph in the end, or love will be the last word, or something similar. Revelation, on this view, certainly occurs through contact with the Bible, but the communicated content is only a slice of the Bible; in particular, the event of revelation does not necessarily lead to a positive avowing of apostolic theology, as such, as divine truth, or to any clear link between the doctrine of grace and Christian ethical imperatives comparable to that which we find in the epistles of Paul. This outlook is not unlike that of the old Continental Liberalism, which was based, not on Platonism, but on mysticism framed by historical positivism. Both views in practice by-pass the apostles and concentrate on the Jesus of the gospels as teacher, pioneer, and example of the good life.

By contrast, 'dialectical' theologians like Brunner, and Niebuhr, have held that the Word of God in Christ with which the Bible confronts us is a reality which has to be set forth in the categories of apostolic teaching about sin and salvation – though this, they would have said, does not oblige us to echo the apostles at every point, since details of the apostolic witness to the Word of God sometimes need recasting and improving. Those in this camp would all say that Jesus Christ rather than Scripture is the Word of God (an improper antithesis, as we saw); but if we ask them, on that basis, to give us an account of Jesus Christ, and to tell us how the two Testaments belong together, and how the Christ of apostolic faith stands related to the Jesus of historical fact, their unanimity dissolves at once into a shambles of conflicts and confusions.

A third, 'existentialist', type of view, popularized earlier this century by the work of Bultmann and Tillich, is that the Word of God is, strictly speaking, neither Holy Scripture nor Jesus Christ, but God confronting individuals in a way which produces within them a liberating assurance, assuaging their otherwise incurable *angst* (restless anxiety). This assurance – 'openness to the future', Bultmann called it – was equated with faith. It does not come, said its exponents, without our contemplating the (largely unhistorical and mythological) New Testament witness to Jesus, but it is none the less consistent with denying Jesus' personal deity, pre-existence, virgin birth, miracles, bodily resurrection, and indeed every bit of information about Him that the New Testament gives us save the bare fact that He was crucified.

It is clear that such 'faith' is not very different from the unfocused cosmic optimism of the Anglican 'broad church' outlook – which perhaps helps to explain how the author of *Honest to God* could feel at home with Bultmann and Tillich, and even hail the oracular but vacuous abstractions of Bultmann's letter to the Sheffield Industrial Mission, setting out his 'demythologized' version of the Gospel, as an example of 'profound simplicity'.[3] Indeed, analysis shows that the modern 'broad church', liberal, and existentialist positions, however superficially different, are all really members of the same theological family. They are all versions of what we may call Renaissance theology, the Erasmian type of thought within Protestantism. Renaissance theology is characteristically rationalistic, anti-dogmatic, and agnostic in temper, ethical and humanitarian in its interests, and ready to hail almost any kind of religious outlook and belief about God (and some moderns have added in certain types of atheism too) as having in it the substance of Christian faith, so long as it recognizes the absoluteness of Christian moral values. Between, on the one hand, Renaissance theology and, on the other, the Reformed and 'Catholic' traditions, which agree at least in holding that Christian faith involves believing the Creed, so great a gulf is fixed that both evangelicals and 'catholics' often find themselves unable to treat teaching of the Renaissance type as Christian at all. Certainly, as both these schools within the Church of England stressed a century ago, when faced with *Essays and Reviews*, and as both have stressed again more recently in face of *Honest to God*, our formularies make it impossible to regard any type of Renaissance theology as other than a cuckoo in the Anglican nest.

Cuckoos, however, grow to considerable size, and Renaissance theology has recently been 'in' in a big way in the Church of England. The most popular form of it centres on the thought that Jesus, though a fine man whose life was an act of God in a special way, was not the second person of the Trinity incarnate, for God is not, strictly speaking, tripersonal at all. Into this revamped unitarianism the concept 'Word of

God' hardly entered: the New Testament witness to Jesus Christ was read in Bultmann's way, as unhistorical myth, all thought of revealed truth was dismissed, and Christian faith was reduced to a sense of ultimate value in Jesus' manner of life, as a model for imitation and a way of actually tuning in to God. Whether such threadbare theology can last long is doubtful, but in books like Dennis Nineham's *The Use and Abuse of the Bible* (1976), Maurice Wiles' *The Remaking of Christian Doctrine* (1974), Don Cupitt's *Jesus and the Gospel of God* (1976), and the symposium, *The Myth of God Incarnate* (1977), and more recently the American John Spong's *Rescuing The Bible from Fundamentalism* (1991) and *Born of a Woman* (1992), it has certainly had a good innings.

Of all these varieties of Renaissance theology, and with them the cross-bred 'dialectical theology', which has one foot in the Reformation camp and the other in the Renaissance camp, and shifts its weight from foot to foot according to who expounds it, three things have to be said. First, these positions are all *subjectivist* in character – that is, they all depend on denying at some point the correlation between Scripture and faith, biblical revelation and inward illumination, the Spirit in the Scriptures and the Spirit in the heart, and on appealing to the latter to justify forsaking the former. In other words, one only reaches them by backing at some point one's private view of what the Bible is, or should be, driving against what it actually says, and jettisoning in practice part of what it teaches in order to maintain this private opinion. In principle and method, these subjectivist positions all part company with both Reformation and 'Catholic' theology to line up with the sixteenth-century Anabaptists and seventeenth-century Quakers, who held that the 'internal word' or 'inner light' justified them in sitting loose to 'God's Word written'.

Second, these positions are all *unstable*, for they recognize no objective criterion of truth, nor method for establishing it, save the more or less speculative reasoning of individual theologians, whose conclusions never command full agreement within their own camp, let alone outside it. The pendulum keeps swinging all the time; systems rise and fall; theological fashions, like fashions in the styling of cars or ladies' hats, rapidly come and go. The first quarter of this century was the age of liberalism, dominated by Troeltsch and Harnack; the second quarter was the age of dialecticism, dominated by Brunner and Barth; the third quarter was the age of existentialism, dominated by Bultmann and Tillich; the fourth quarter has been the age of liberation theologies, chiefly Latin American, black and feminist; the twenty-first century will no doubt see other fashionable 'isms', and other dominant thinkers rising and falling. The truth is that the world of Renaissance theology is a desert of continually shifting sand, where stability is impossible. Listening to the babel of Renaissance theologians' voices, confident though they often are, one soon sees that there is no hope of reaching certainty about anything in such company. Relativism is the ruling principle; every question goes back again and again into the melting-pot; syntheses are merely provisional, and the state of flux is never-ending.

Third, so far as they fail to uphold the authority of the Spirit in the Scriptures over the Spirit in the theologian, and deviate from the task of expounding and applying what the Bible actually says, these positions are really *sub-Christian*; as the rest of this chapter will show.

GOD-BREATHED SCRIPTURE

We come now to state in outline what we take to be the true view, as it is certainly the historic Anglican view, of the Holy Scriptures. Traditionally it has been summed up by calling the Bible, as in the marriage service, 'God's Word', or, as in Article XX, 'God's Word written'. The value of such phraseology is that it at once indicates, first, that what Scripture says, God says (the Word *of God*); second, that the Scriptures together make up a total presentation of God's message to mankind (*the* Word of God); third, that the Scriptures constitute a message addressed directly by God to everyone who reads or hears them (the *Word* of God) – in other words, that the Scriptures have the nature of *preaching*. The 'Word of the Lord' conveyed by the prophets in their oracles, and the 'Word of God' set forth by the apostles in their sermons, was always a word applying directly to its hearers, summoning them to recognize that God Himself was thereby addressing them, calling on them to respond to His instruction and direction, and working in them through God's own Spirit to evoke the response which it required (cf. I Thess. 2:13). Similarly, the Bible as a whole, viewed from the standpoint of its contents, should be thought of, not statically, but dynamically; not merely as what God said long ago, but as what He says still; and not merely as what He says to men in general, but as what He says to each individual reader or hearer in particular. In other words, Holy Scripture should be thought of as *God preaching* – God preaching to me every time I read or hear any part of it – God the Father preaching God the Son in the power of God the Holy Spirit. God the Father is the giver of Holy Scripture; God the Son is the theme of Holy Scripture; and God the Spirit, as the Father's appointed agent in witnessing to the Son, is the author, authenticator, and interpreter, of Holy Scripture. This is the position which we shall now try to elucidate, by means of some further study of what biblical inspiration implies.

We saw in the last chapter what inspiration was in the prophets: a divine work, taking many psychological forms, whereby, having made God's message known to them, the Holy Spirit so overruled all their subsequent mental activity in giving the message poetic and literary form that each resultant oracle was as truly a divine utterance as a human, as direct a disclosure of what was in God's mind as of what was in the prophet's. Also, we saw that the New Testament extends this concept of dual authorship to cover all the Old Testament, second-person psalms of address to God (cf. Heb. 1:8-12, 2:6ff.) or admonitions from the wise man to his pupil (cf. Heb. 12:5f), and third-person narratives of God's words and doings, as well as first-person divine utterances spoken through prophetic messengers. Our Lord quotes the narrator's marginal comment in Genesis 2:24 as what 'the Creator . . . said' (Mt. 19:4f.). Paul tells the Corinthian Christians that the history of Israel's wilderness wanderings was 'written down as warnings for us, on whom the fulfilment of the ages has come' (I Cor. 10:11; cf. Rom. 15:4). Paul also calls the

Old Testament as a whole 'the very words of God' (Rom.
3:2; cf. Acts 7:38), and twice says 'Scripture' when he means
'God, as recorded in Scripture' ('the Scripture foresaw . . .
announced . . .' [Gal 3:8]; 'the Scripture says to Pharaoh: "I
raised you up for this very purpose,"' [Rom. 9:17]). Thus he
shows that for him biblical statements were, quite simply,
words of God talking about Himself. Similarly, in Romans
4 and Galatians 3:6ff., Paul treats what 'the Scripture says'
about Abraham (that he 'believed God, and it was credited
to him as righteousness') as divine testimony to the way of
salvation. The New Testament concept of Old Testament
inspiration is crystallized in the statement in II Timothy 3:16,
'all Scripture is God-breathed' (*theopneustos*, literally 'breathed
out from God'). The thought here is that, just as God made the
host of heaven 'by the breath of his mouth' (Ps. 33:6), through
His own creative fiat, so we should regard the Scriptures as
the product of a similar creative fiat – 'let there be Law,
Prophets, and Writings' (the three divisions of the Jewish
canon in New Testament times). The New Testament faith
about the Old Testament was that the real narrator of
Israel's history in the Law and Former Prophets (that is,
the Pentateuch and historical books), and the real psalmist,
poet, and wisdom-teacher in the Writings, as well as the
real preacher of the prophets' sermons, was God Himself.

Moreover, we have also seen that our Lord, according
to His own explicit testimony, spoke from God, and so did
His apostles, to whom He promised His Spirit to enable
them to do precisely this in their witness to Himself (see Jn.
14:26, 15:26f., 16:7-15, 20:21ff.; cf. Mt. 10:19f.; Lk. 10:16;
I Cor. 2:12f.). Apostolic witness to Christ, spoken or written,
thus has the same Spirit-prompted, divine-human character
– that is, is inspired in the same sense – as the sacred books
of the Old Testament. As, therefore, we should follow the
New Testament Christians in viewing the Old Testament as
given by God for our learning, so we should read the New
Testament as part of Jesus Christ's legacy to us – as if at each
point we heard Him say, 'I had Paul (or John, or Matthew,
or whoever it is) write this in order to help *you*'. This is what
it means to believe in biblical inspiration biblically.

The inspiring process, which brought each writer's thoughts into such exact coincidence with those of God, necessarily involved a unique oversight and control of those who were its subjects. Some moderns doubt whether this control could leave room for any free mental activity on the writers' part, and pose a dilemma: *either* God's control of the writers was complete, in which case they wrote as robots or automata (which clearly they did not), *or* their minds worked freely as they wrote the Scriptures, in which case God could not fully have controlled them, or kept them from error. Exponents of this dilemma usually hold that the evidence for errors (false statements purporting to be true) in the Bible is in fact as conclusive as the evidence for spontaneous self-expression by its human writers. But our first comment must be that this is not so. That Scripture errs has been assumed by many, but it cannot in principle be proved, any more than it can be proved that Jesus was not morally perfect. Both questions are actually settled farther back: if Jesus was God incarnate, He could not but be morally perfect, and if Scripture is the Word of the God of truth it cannot but be true and trustworthy at all points. Moreover, the dilemma rests on the assumption that full psychological freedom of thought and action, and full subjection to divine control, are incompatible; and this is not true either. If the inspiration of the prophets was what all Scriptures say it was, it is absurd to deny that the whole Bible could be similarly inspired.

Instead of imposing on God arbitrary limitations of this sort, we should rather adore the wisdom and power that could so order the unruly minds of sinful men as to cause them freely and spontaneously, with no inhibiting of their normal mental processes, to write only and wholly the infallible truth of God. As B. B. Warfield observed, we are not to imagine that when God wanted Paul's letters written 'He was reduced to the necessity of going down to the earth and painfully scrutinizing the men He found there, seeking anxiously for the one who, on the whole, promised best for His purpose; and then violently forcing the material he wished expressed through him, against his natural bent, and with as little loss from his recalcitrant characteristics as possible. Of course, nothing of the sort took place. If God wished to give His people a series of letters like Paul's, He prepared a Paul to write them, and the Paul He brought to the task was a Paul who spontaneously would write just such letters.'4 Of course – but what a marvel of providential management this was! And, for that matter, what a marvel of condescending mercy it was that God should speak to men at all! And what patience and skill He showed throughout the long history of revelation in always so adapting His message to the capacities of His chosen messengers that it never overran their powers of transmission, but within the limits set by their mind, outlook, culture, language, and literary ability, could always find adequate and exact expression! But such gracious self-limitation is typical of the God of Bethlehem's stable and Calvary's cross.

Inspiration took many psychological forms; here, as elsewhere, God showed Himself a God of variety. The basic form of the process was *dualistic* inspiration, in which the recipient of revelation remained conscious throughout of the distinction between himself, the hearer and reporter, and God, the Speaker to and through him. The inspiration that produced the Old Testament prophetic oracles, including the Mosaic legislation and the apocalyptic visions of Daniel and John the divine, was of this kind. But there were other forms, too, in which this consciousness was not present, so that the human authors may well not have been aware of being inspired, in the strict sense of the word, at all. There was, on the one hand, *lyric* inspiration, in which the inspiring action of God was fused with the concentrating, intensifying, and shaping mental processes of what, in the secular sense, we would call the inspiration of the poet. This produced the Psalms, the lyrical drama of Job (which as it stands is a highly wrought theological poem, whatever basis it may be thought to have in historical fact), the Song of Solomon (a parable of the love of God and His people, in the form of an exotic, erotic, ecstatic love-duet), and the many great prayers that we find scattered through the historical books. Then, on the other hand, there were various forms of *organic* or *didactic* inspiration, whereby the inspiring action of God coalesced with the mental processes – enquiring, analytical, reflective, interpretative, applicatory – of the teacher, seeking to distil and pass on knowledge of facts and right thoughts about them. This type of inspiration produced the historical books of both Testaments, the apostolic letters, and, in the Old Testament, the books of Proverbs and Ecclesiastes. There was, of course, nothing to prevent the same man being the medium at different times of different forms of divine inspiration, and it seems clear that all three were combined in the highest degree in the inspiration of our Lord Himself. The importance of these observations lies in the fact that to recognize what form of inspiration each biblical passage displays is always the first essential for interpreting it soundly.

BIBLICAL AUTHORITY

We are now in a position to take up the vexed issue of the authority of Scripture. Authority, the right to rule, belongs ultimately to God the Creator, and Christianity is ultimately a matter of bowing to His authority by obedient response to His revelation. On this formula all Christians agree. All, therefore, acknowledge Scripture, the written record of God's revelation, as in some sense authoritative for faith and life. But when we ask, in what sense, agreement ends, and conflicts begin. A clear grasp, however, of the meaning of biblical inspiration, as set forth above, will go far to guide us through these tangles of controversy.

The first problem that arises concerns *the nature of biblical authority*. Liberal Protestants, viewing the Bible as no more than fallible human witness to the revelatory process, and doubtful whether that process really involved divine speech to man, or whether any Scripture statements can be taken as actual utterances of God, build their concept of biblical authority in terms of three thoughts: first, the necessity of the Bible, as the only source of knowledge about God's revelatory acts; second, the quality of the Bible, as a testament of deep religious experience; third, the potency of the Bible, proved down the centuries, to bring moral and spiritual uplift to all sorts and conditions of men. On this basis, as is plain, questions like: Did all the things which Scripture records happen as recorded? Did the biblical writers' thoughts express true insight at every point? Can every part of the Bible yield genuine instruction and guidance today? still remain open, and it is in fact assumed from the start that, the Bible being, for all its religious and theological expertise, a merely human book, the answer to all three questions is probably no. This approach makes the theologian appear, willy-nilly, as a sort of salvage man, using the criteria of modern mental culture to pick out what is of value from the mass of miscellaneous antique matter that the Bible contains. Also, it puts him on the defensive, making him hesitant and apologetic whenever, following Scripture, he ventures to affirm the supernatural, as if he expects every minute to be told by a colleague that the items he has selected from the mass were not really worth much. The substance of the common liberal complaint that conservative evangelicals give too little place to reason in formulating the doctrine of authority seems only to be a feeling of injury and offence that evangelicals do not approach these questions with the same negative presuppositions, nor show the same deference to the axioms and attitudes of unbelief.

But this whole approach is incorrect, for it views biblical authority in purely human, relative terms, whereas in fact, as the doctrine of inspiration makes plain, the authority of Scripture is the divine authority of God Himself speaking. The Bible is not only man's word, but God's also; not merely a record of revelation, but a written revelation in its own right, God's own witness to Himself in the form of human witness to Him. Accordingly, the authority of the Scriptures rests, not simply on their worth as an historical source, a testament of religion, and a means of uplift, real though this is, but primarily and essentially on the fact that they come to us from the mouth of God. Therefore the real task for reason in this connection is not to try to censure and correct the Scriptures, but rather, with God's help, to try to understand and apply them, so that God may effectively censure and correct us.

But, it is objected, does not the Christian stand directly under the authority of the Lord Jesus Christ, and is not Jesus Christ Lord also of the Scriptures? And if so, how can the

Christian be said to be bound to the authority of the Bible? The answer is very simple. The antithesis is a false one. Jesus Christ is Lord of the Scriptures in the same sense in which any absolute monarch is Lord of the laws and proclamations which he sees fit to issue for the government of his subjects. The ruler's laws carry his personal authority, and the measure of one's loyalty to him is the consistency of one's observance of them. But Holy Scripture, 'the sceptre of God', as Calvin somewhere calls it, is Christ's instrument of government: it comes to us, so to speak, from His hand and with His seal upon it, for He Himself commended the Old Testament to us as having His Father's authority,[5] and He Himself authorized and empowered the apostles to speak in His name, by His Spirit and with His own authority.[6] So the way to bow to the authority of Jesus Christ is precisely by bowing to the authority of the inspired Scriptures.

BIBLICAL INTERPRETATION

But a second problem now arises. Granted that biblical teaching, because it is divine teaching, must be our rule of faith and life, *how are we to interpret the Bible* and extract its teaching from it?

We cannot here answer this question as it deserves, for that would take a book; what we can do, however, is to show that the guiding principles for interpreting Scripture all follow from the doctrine of inspiration.

Interpretation, says J. D. Wood, is 'the way of reading an ancient book in order that it may become relevant to the life and thought of a later day'.[7] If the Bible is the divine-human product we take it to be, then the interpreting of it involves three distinct activities: *exegesis*, *synthesis*, and *application*. We will say a word about each.

Because the Bible is a human book, God having chosen to convey His teaching to us in the form of the inspired instruction of His human penmen, the way into His mind is necessarily *via* their minds. So the basic discipline in biblical interpretation must always be exegetical analysis – that is, the attempt to determine as exactly as possible just what the

writer meant by the words he wrote, and how he would explain the sense of his statements could we cross-question him
about them. Exegesis involves, on the one hand, setting each
passage against its external background (historical, cultural,
geographical, linguistic, literary), and, on the other hand,
determining from its intrinsic characteristics its aim, scope,
standpoint, presuppositions, and range and limit of interest.
The first part of this task may call for a good deal of technical
learning, but this does not mean that exegesis is work for
scholars only; the decisive part of the task is the second part,
for which the first is, at most, only ground-clearing, and in
this the professional scholar does not stand on any higher
footing than any diligent student of the text in any language.
The supreme requirement for understanding a biblical book –
or, indeed, any other human document – is sympathy with its
subject-matter, and a mind and heart that can spontaneously
enter into the author's outlook. But the capacity to put oneself
in the shoes of Isaiah, or Paul, or John, and see with his eyes
and feel with his heart is the gift, not of academic training,
but of the Holy Spirit through the new birth.

To take the measure of the mind of each biblical prophet,
apostle, historian, psalmist, and wisdom writer, might seem
work enough in itself; but in fact exegetical analysis is only
the beginning of the interpretative task. Because the Bible is a
divine book as well as a human one, and because the sixty-six
separate documents that make it up, under all their human
diversity, are products of a single divine mind setting forth
a single message, it is necessary to proceed from exegesis to
synthesis, and to seek to integrate the fruit of our study of
the individual books and writers into a single coherent whole.
We come to the task of exegesis with the knowledge that all
the human author's thoughts concerning God are God's own
thoughts too; but when we move on to the further task of
synthesis, we soon become aware that at point after point
God's thoughts go further and embrace more than those of
any one biblical writer did or could. The full significance of
each passage only appears when it is set in the context of all
the rest of Scripture – which its own author, of course, was
never able to do. The Bible appears like a symphony orchestra,

with the Holy Spirit as its Toscanini; each instrumentalist has been brought willingly, spontaneously, creatively, to play his notes just as the great conductor desired, in full harmony with each other, though none of them could ever hear the music as a whole. Not only the prophets who foretold Christ (cf. I Pet. 1:10-12), but all the writers of both Testaments, are constantly telling us more than ever they themselves knew. The point of each part only becomes fully clear when seen in relation to all the rest.

In this task of synthesis, the guiding principle must be the self-consistency of Scripture, in other words the principle that in giving us the Bible the Holy Spirit did not contradict Himself. The Reformers called this axiom 'the analogy of faith'. As they understood it, it was really three principles in one. It was, first, the principle of working from the centre outwards, explaining what is secondary by the light of what is primary, and what is obscure in terms of what is clear. This in practice meant – and means – recognizing that the central themes of the Bible are the kingdom, people, and covenant of God, and the person, place, work, and glory, of the Lord Jesus Christ; the achieving, and applying of redemption; the law and the Gospel. Second, the Reformers' phrase signified the principle of following out the inner links of Scripture. This meant, for instance, understanding Old Testament prophecy in the light of the New Testament account of its fulfilment, understanding types in the light of their antitypes, understanding Leviticus in the light of Hebrews, and the doings of Old Testament characters in the light of New Testament comment on them. Third, 'the analogy of faith' meant the principle of understanding Scripture harmonistically, not setting text against text or supposing apparent contradictions to be real ones, but seeking rather to let one passage throw light on another, in the certainty that there is in Scripture a perfect agreement between part and part, which careful study will be able to bring out. The Anglican Articles apply this principle twice. With our Lord (Jn. 5:39, 46), Paul (Rom. 4), and the writer to the Hebrews (*passim*), and against sixteenth-century Anabaptists and, along with them, earlier Marcionites and later liberals and dispensationalists, Article VII affirms that 'the Old Testament is not contrary to the New; for both in the Old and New Testament everlasting life is offered to Mankind through Christ . . .' Also, Article XX states that, 'although the (visible) Church be a witness and a keeper of holy Writ', it may not 'so expound one place of Scripture, that it be repugnant to another' – for such exposition must be wrong.

So, then, to take one example, it would not be right to dismiss the imprecatory Psalms in the way that many do, as vindictive outbursts contrary to the mind of God, expressing the vengeful spirit which the New Testament condemns. The Homilies themselves warn us against this mistake. The truth is that what Psalms like 35, 58, 109, and 137:7-9 are voicing is a zeal and passion for God's glory, and for the triumph of His cause and His righteousness, which far exceeds ours, in the same way that Psalms 17:1-5, 26:1-5, and 131 express a humility and simplicity of spirit that is far above our own. Just as, had we written the words of these latter Psalms, they would have argued priggishness and conceit, and the words of triumph-songs like Judges 5, Isaiah 47 and Revelation 19:1-3, had they been our words, would have savoured of gloating, so too the words of the cursing Psalms, had we spoken them, would have revealed an all-too-human ill-will. But this only means that our hearts are less pure than the hearts of the psalmists. David, writes the homilist, 'spake them [the imprecations] not of a private hatred, and in a stomach against their persons; but wished spiritually the destruction of such corrupt errors and vices, which reigned in all devilish persons set against God . . . he hated the wicked . . . with a perfect hate (Ps. 139:21f.), not with a malicious hate to the hurt of the soul. Which perfection of spirit, because it cannot be performed in us, so corrupted in affections as we be, we ought not to use in our private causes the like form in words, for that we cannot fulfil the like words in sense . . .' ('An Information for them which take Offence at certain places of the Holy Scripture': *The Homilies*, pp. 382f.). Thus the truth is that here, no less than at other points, the psalmist is expressing true devotion at its highest pitch, and the fancied disharmony between his words and New Testament ideals does not exist. In fact, the same spirit is voiced in the New Testament also: see Rev. 6:10.

Therefore the attitude of those who decline to use these verses from God's hymn-book in public worship seems doubtfully wise. Is it not good for us to be shown, even if we can hardly at present grasp, what true zeal for God's honour is like?[8]

The third part of the work of interpretation is to apply biblical teaching to ourselves, individually and corporately. It is here most of all that we need the help of the Spirit who inspired the Scriptures to give us understanding. God-inspired Scripture, writes Paul, 'is useful for teaching, rebuking, correcting and training in righteousness' (II Tim. 3:16); but we cannot reap this profit till the Spirit quickens our minds and consciences to measure and judge ourselves by Scripture, and to discern the issues of repentance, and faith, and obedience, and amending of our ways, which across the centuries Holy Scripture forces upon us. Here, again, the decisive qualification is not academic scholarship, but rather a praying, humble, teachable heart. The rule that applies is that to him that hath shall be given: it is only as we obey God up to the limit of our present insight into His will that our insight will be deepened and our vision enlarged. Live by the light you have as to the bearing of Scripture on your life, and you shall have more light; neglect the light you have, and you will actually darken it, so that in the outcome you will have less. This solemn alternative faces every Christian every day of his or her life.

It is obvious that in practice all three parts of the task of biblical interpretation will, and must, be carried on together, and that deepened insight at any one stage will result in deeper insight at the other two stages also. It is obvious too that the enterprise may break down at any of its three stages. It seems clear that in present-day Protestantism it has largely broken down at all three stages. Unwillingness to take seriously the biblical writers' thoughts as being, strictly and precisely, the communicated thoughts of God; unwillingness to be led and bound by the analogy of faith in unifying the fruits of exegesis; and indolence in seeking to apply to human life what the Bible actually says – these are the root causes of our 'famine of hearing the words of the Lord'. And there is no hope of the famine being alleviated till these things are penitently put right.

The kind of interpretation that results when these principles are properly applied can be sampled in the work of such people as John Chrysostom (fifth century), John Calvin (sixteenth century), Matthew Henry (seventeenth century), John Charles Ryle (nineteenth century), and Dr Martyn Lloyd-Jones (twentieth century): five who would have hailed each other as blood-brothers in faith had they met (and who of course in heaven may already have done so). Those today who are hungry for the Lord's words are guaranteed nourishment if they turn to these classic expositors.

INFALLIBLE? INERRANT?

When Thomas Hobbes declared that 'words are the counters of wise men, they do reckon by them; but they are the coinage of fools', he was warning us that words, being tools of thought and tokens of meaning, are neither magical nor impregnable, and we abuse our minds if we think otherwise. Anything you really understand you can express in more than one form of words, and no verbal formula is exempt from the possibility of reinterpretation, misinterpretation and debasement by those who come after its framers. It is well to remind ourselves of this as we weigh two words which twentieth-century English-speaking theologians have regularly applied to the view of Scripture as God-given verbal revelation which this book has been setting forth. The words are *infallibility* and *inerrancy*, both denoting qualities which adherents of this view ascribe to the Bible.

The first thing to say, in the light of the last paragraph, is that nobody should feel wedded to these words. We can get on without them. If we speak of Holy Scripture as altogether true and trustworthy, or as wholly reliable in its own terms, making no false assertions, claims or promises on its own account (however many lies told by good men, bad men and devils it records), we shall be expressing in formula terms exactly what these words mean. If we prefer these formulae to the words themselves (both of which, be it admitted, have turned into noses of wax, malleable and often misshapen in recent discussion), that is our privilege, and none should want to deprive us of it. Conversely, adherence to traditional terms does not necessarily argue the profoundest grasp of what they stand for; it may only be a sign of a traditional mind.

Yet this is an age in which the view I am stating is often dismissed without argument, and indeed without understanding, as an assertion of 'verbal infallibility' or 'verbal inerrancy' (uncouth phrases! Why 'verbal'? What other sort of infallibility or inerrancy might there be?). In such an age, it is more useful to explain and defend the words, and rebut the criticisms, than to renounce the words because they have been mishandled. Rightly understood, they are useful theological shorthand, and by explaining them we can clarify and develop some of the implications of what this chapter has said so far. Briefly, then (or as briefly as we can!):

First, their *meaning*. *Infallibility* is the Latin *infallibilitas*, signifying the quality of neither deceiving nor being deceived. *Inerrancy* is the Latin *inerrantia*, meaning freedom from error of any kind, factual, moral or spiritual. *Infallible* as a description of the biblical Word of God goes back at least to the English Reformation.[9] *Inerrant* is an adjective that gained currency in the second half of the last century, in debates that arose from the budding 'higher criticism'. Both words take colour from the contexts in which they were mainly used; thus, though they are virtually synonyms, *infallible* suggests to most minds Scripture determining a faith-commitment, while *inerrant* evokes rather the thought of Scripture undergirding an orthodoxy. But for practical purposes the words are interchangeable.

Second, their *significance*. Though negative in form, they are positive in thrust, like the Council of Chalcedon's four negative adverbs about the union of Christ's two natures in His one person ('without confusion', 'without change', 'without division', 'without separation'). What those adverbs say is that only within the limits they set is truth about the incarnation found. What *infallible* and *inerrant* say is that only those who accept as from God all that Scripture proves to tell us, promise us or require of us can ever fully please Him. Both words thus have religious as well as theological significance; their function is to impose on our handling of

the Bible a procedure which expresses faith in the reality and
veracity of the God who speaks to us in and through what it
says and who requires us to heed every word that proceeds
from His mouth. The procedure, best stated negatively, is
that in exegesis and exposition of Scripture and building
up our biblical theology we may not (i) deny, disregard, or
arbitrarily relativize anything that the writers teach, nor (ii)
discount any of the practical implications for worship and
service which their teaching carries, nor (iii) cut the knot
of any problem of Bible harmony, factual or theological,
by allowing ourselves to assume that the writers were not
necessarily consistent with themselves or with each other. It is
this procedure, rather than any particular results of following
it, that our two words safeguard.

Third, their *justification*. The ground for affirming that
Scripture is infallible and inerrant is its inspiration, which we
defined earlier in this chapter in terms of God-breathedness
or divine origin. No Christian will question that God speaks
truth and truth only (that is, that what He says is infallible
and inerrant). But if all Scripture comes from God in such a
sense that what it says, He says, then Scripture as such must
be infallible and inerrant, because it is God's utterance. What
our two words express is not confidence that by our own
independent enquiries we can prove all Scripture statements
to be true (we can't, of course, and should never speak as if
we could), but certainty that all Scripture can and should be
trusted because it has come to us (in Calvin's phrase) 'by the
ministry of men from God's very mouth'.[10]

Fourth, how these words are *misunderstood*. Critics per-
sistently suppose that both words, highlighting as they do
the divinity and consequent truth of the Bible, express or
entail a policy of minimizing the Bible's humanity, either by
denying its human literary sources or ignoring the marks of
its human cultural milieu, or by treating it as if it were written
in terms of the communicative techniques and conventions
of the modern West rather than the ancient East, or by
professing to find in it 'technical-scientific' as distinct from
'naive-observational' statements about the natural order,
when the 'technical-scientific' study of nature is less than

five centuries old. It is understandable that Christians who have not weighed the differences between our culture and that (or those!) of the biblical period should naively feel that the natural and straightforward way to express their certainty that the contents of Scripture, being divine, are of contemporary relevance (as they certainly are) is to treat Scripture as contemporary in its literary forms. No doubt many have done this, believing that thus they did God service. But our words have no link with this naivety; they express no advance commitment of any kind in the field of biblical interpretation, save that whatever Scripture, rightly interpreted (interpreted, that is, *a posteriori*, with linguistic correctness, in terms of the discernible literary character of each book, against its own historical and cultural background, and in the light of its topical relation to other books), proves to be saying should be reverently received, as from God.

Fifth, the *self-involving logic* of these words. For me to confess that Scripture is infallible and inerrant is to bind myself in advance to follow the method of harmonizing and integrating all that Scripture declares, without remainder, of taking it as from God, however little I may like it, and whatever change of present beliefs, ways and commitments it may require, and of seeking actively to live by it. Both words are often seen as belonging to worlds of doctrinaire scholasticism, but in fact they express a most radical existential commitment on the Christian's part.

Sixth, the *objections* to these words. Some deprecate them because using them, they think, has a bad effect. Affirming *inerrancy* is thought to cause preoccupation with minutiae of Bible harmony and factual detail to the neglect of major matters, and to encourage the unhistorical kind of exegesis that we glanced at two paragraphs back, and thus to thwart good scholarship. Asserting *infallibility* is held to spawn a superstitious bibliolatry which reveres the Bible as a sort of everyman's-enquire-within-about-everything, and also thwarts good scholarship. It may be replied that none of this is necessarily so, and that it is worth disinfecting both words from association with these failures in responsible biblical interpretation. But if it is still thought best to eschew the terms as tainted, the point is not worth pressing; as we said, we are not wedded to words. Others, however, reject the terms on the grounds that factual, moral, and theological error in the Bible is now proven. Here I must limit myself simply to replying: not so at all. A responsible biblical scholarship exists with inerrancy as one of its methodological presuppositions; it appears no less successful in embracing and making sense of the phenomena of Scripture than is the scholarship which lacks this presupposition. (All scholars, of course, borrow from and interact with each other, and share a community feeling in consequence, whatever their presuppositions, but that is not the point here.) As long as a consistent Bible-believing scholarship can maintain itself in debate on problem passages, it is sheer triumphalist obscurantism to say that error in the Bible has been proved. And even if adequate Bible-believing scholarship were lacking, 'proved' would still be too strong a word, for the various sceptical hypotheses are never the only ones possible.[11]

THE SUFFICIENCY OF SCRIPTURE

What we have said so far in this chapter might well lower our stock in the eyes of many liberal and 'broad church' Anglicans, but would, we think, command the substantial assent of most Anglo-Catholics, and with them members of the Roman and Orthodox communions too. But now we come to the third problem in connection with biblical authority, the question of *the sufficiency of Scripture*, and here we reach the second great parting of the ways in connection with our view of the Bible.[12] The so-called 'Catholic' (as opposed to 'Reformed') tradition, in all its forms, holds that Holy Scripture, interpreted in terms of itself, is not sufficient as a guide for those who would live under the authority of God. Church tradition is necessary (it is said) to lead us into the right understanding of the Scriptures, which is not accessible from a straightforward study of the text. True, holders of this position disagree among themselves as to what 'Church tradition' is. The Roman Catholic Council of Trent spoke of unwritten apostolic traditions, passed on orally in the Church down the ages, as being a second source of doctrine alongside the Scriptures – a fact which embarrasses many modern Roman theologians, who prefer to work with a dynamic, 'open-ended' concept of tradition as the word of God in the hearts of the (Roman) faithful, constantly crystallizing out through the Spirit's stimulus into consensus of opinion which is then at point after point infallibly recorded in successive papal definitions. Anglo-Catholic and Orthodox teachers, by contrast, make use of an organic but circumscribed idea of tradition as, in general, the developed faith and outlook of the universal Church during the first centuries of its life and, in particular, its sacraments, creeds, Scriptures, and ministers, and its convictions about each. Detailed differences between these groups spring directly from their differing views of tradition, but these need not delay us. What concerns us at present is simply the fact that 'Catholics' of every sort unite against 'Reformed' Christians in insisting that tradition is more than the Scriptures, that the Scriptures are only part of the authoritative legacy of the past that must determine our faith, and that therefore they may not be detached from the rest of tradition and set to judge it, but must themselves be construed in harmony with it; for what tradition says is what Scripture must mean, and if we take it to mean anything contrary we necessarily misunderstand it.[13]

Thus, when 'Catholics' say (as in these days many of them are ready, perhaps too ready, to do) that the Bible is our authoritative rule of faith, what they mean is that our standard of truth must be the interpretation of the Bible which tradition gives us   which is not necessarily that interpretation at which one would arrive by simply comparing Scripture with Scripture. Endless confusion arises in discussion with 'Catholics', as modern ecumenical theology makes painfully apparent, when it is not seen that what they and what 'Reformed' Christians mean by biblical authority are two quite different things.

The issue here is whether Holy Scripture, as a written revelation from God, is in itself complete, clear, and decisive, as a rule for our faith and life, or not. On this question the Church of England took a firm and unambiguous stand four centuries ago. Article VI of the Thirty-Nine affirms the sufficiency of Scripture alone as a rule of faith. 'Holy Scripture containeth all things necessary to salvation; so that whatsoever is not read therein, nor may be proved thereby, is not to be required of any man, that it should be believed as an article of the Faith . . .' Article VIII follows this up by telling us that the most venerable and time-honoured products of tradition – the Apostles', Nicene, and Athanasian Creeds – are to be taken as true, not just because they are traditional, but because 'they may be proved by most certain warrants of Holy Scripture'. It is not denied that the ecumenical creeds offer themselves as a guide to the interpretation of Holy Scripture; what is denied, however, is that we may lawfully accept them in that capacity without first testing them by those very Scriptures whose substance they seek to set forth. For the creeds, like the decisions of all popes, councils, and individual churches (see Articles XIX, XXI), are the work of sinful men, to whom no personal infallibility was ever promised; therefore they must be verified by appeal to what the homilist calls God's 'infallible Word' (we cited him above, p.36), and not seen as themselves an 'infallible word' which should control our interpretation of Scripture. The presupposition of our formularies is that Holy Scripture, interpreted from within itself in the manner which we have described, by means of grammatico-historical exegesis and the analogy of faith, constitutes a clear, definite, and obligatory rule of faith and life, by which all belief and behaviour, corporate and private, must be directed, and to which all controversies between Christians must be brought for settlement.

Such is the historic Anglican position: is it the right one? Unquestionably it is. It rests on two principles. The first is that all Christians of all ages must align themselves with the churches of New Testament times in direct subjection to the doctrinal and practical teaching of the apostles. The apostles were God's chosen and anointed witnesses to Christ (cf. Acts 1:8, 10:39-43). Their teaching, organically linked with the Old Testament, the fulfilment of which they announced, was truth from God, revealed and inspired by Christ's Spirit and set forth in His name and with His authority. As such it forms an authoritative standard of truth and criterion of error, not only for the apostles' own time, but for all time. We find Paul and Peter and John all insisting that hearty acceptance of the teaching they had given, and submission to its authority, is a basic test of true spirituality and godliness, not to mention fitness for the ministry (I Cor. 14:37; II Cor. 11:3f, 13:2-10; Gal. 1:6-9; I Thess. 1:5, 2:13; II Thess. 2:13-15, 3:6-15; II Tim. 2:1f, 3:13f.; Tit. 1:9; II Pet. 1:12-2:3; I Jn. 2:21-24, 4:6; II Jn. 9f.). Were they back among us today, they would still say the same – perhaps even more emphatically! To throw over the authority of apostolic teaching in any degree is, to that extent, a lapse from Christianity. This is the first principle. The second is simply the incontrovertible fact that, as E. A. Litton puts it, 'no apostolical teaching is certainly extant except that which is embalmed in the New Testament'.[14] Hence it follows that the apostolic New Testament, read in conjunction with the Old, of which it is the completion, must always be our final authority and court of appeal. Christ's Church was, and is, to be ruled by His apostles; therefore, by their providentially surviving writings. To say that Christ must be allowed to rule, that the Redeemer must be given His crown rights, is thus to say that Scripture must be allowed to rule, that the Bible must always have the last word.

THE CHURCH AND THE CANON

To turn the flank of this argument, Roman Catholics (not to mention certain Anglicans) are accustomed to argue that the authority of the post-apostolic Church as an on-going, living, Spirit-indwelt community must be prior and superior to that of the New Testament, inasmuch as it was the post-apostolic Church that established the New Testament as a 'canon' – that is, a yardstick – of orthodox faith. But this argument fails. The Church no more gave us the New Testament canon than Sir Isaac Newton gave us the force of gravity. God gave us gravity, by His work of creation, and similarly He gave us the New Testament canon, by inspiring the individual books that make it up. Newton did not create gravity, but recognized it, by considering (so it is said) the fall of an apple;

similarly, the various churches of Christendom, through a gradual, unco-ordinated, seemingly haphazard and erratic process covering several centuries, came to recognize the extent and limits of the God-given canon, by checking and cross-checking the pedigree and contents of the many books that bore apostolic names, or were alleged to proceed from the apostolic circle, to find out which of them could make good their claim to be genuine apostolic products, embodying the revealed truth of which the apostles were trustees. Had one suggested to Christians of the second, third, or fourth century that by this means the Church was creating a canon for itself, choosing out some good-quality Christian literature to authorize as a standard of faith for the future, they would have shaken their heads and marvelled that anyone could dream up an idea so perverse and far from the truth. The belief that apostolic writings, as such, were inspired, and therefore intrinsically authoritative, was the presupposition of their whole inquiry. All that the churches were trying to do was to see which of the books claiming to be in some sufficient sense apostolic really were so – a question primarily of historical fact, though one on which character and content were also held to bear, both positively and negatively.[15]

After three centuries of inquiry, the greater part of Christendom was found to be agreed on its answer to this question, and its agreement was duly recorded by individual theologians and various conciliar decisions (though no conciliar decision, be it noted, was made at any stage to bring agreement into being). Good as the reasons certainly are for thinking that the Spirit, here as elsewhere, had led the Church to a correct discernment, the fact of having been guided to see which books have intrinsic authority can no more be held to give the Church authority over them, to limit their meaning to that which accords with its own tradition, than the fact of my having recognized what came in the post this morning as a genuine bookseller's bill, made out to me, gives me authority over it, to pay only so much of it as I feel inclined to.

A question, however, remains. If we may not ascribe infallibility to the Church's discernment of which books were inspired (and how can we?), then how may we be sure that our New Testament does not contain either too many books or too few? How can we be confident about the limits of the New Testament when we are so poorly placed, nearly two thousand years on, to check the early Church's verdicts about the authorship and authenticity of each item in it? The answer is found by stringing together the following facts.

1. Christianity had both the idea and the reality of canonical Scripture from the start: for Christianity began as a Jewish sect, and Judaism was based on revering what we call the Old Testament as God's *torah* (law, instruction). Jesus confirmed this attitude to His disciples by letting them see that in these Scriptures He recognized His Father's voice, and that under their authority He lived and taught and died, not breaking them but fulfilling them. Naturally, therefore, pioneer missionaries like Paul gave the Old Testament to Gentile churches, which otherwise would not have known it, to function alongside apostolic teaching as their rule of faith and life. 'All Scripture is . . . God-breathed and is useful . . . so that *the man of God*' – the Christian! and in this instance, the minister – 'may be thoroughly equipped for every good work' (2 Tim. 3:16-17). All of it was written 'to teach *us*, so that through . . . the encouragement of the Scriptures *we*' – we Christians! – 'might have hope' (Rom. 15:4; cf. 1 Cor. 10:11). It is basic to Christianity to receive the Old Testament as Christian Scripture.

2. An expectation of new canonical Scripture to stand beside the Old Testament is implicit in the work of God on which Christianity rests. New and climactic revelation came via Jesus to the apostles for the world, and it would have been incomprehensible if the God who caused His earlier revelation to be recorded for posterity had not done the same for that which completed and fulfilled it. When Jesus prayed for the whole Church, apart from the apostles, as those who should 'believe in me through their message' (Jn. 17:20), He assumed permanent availability of that word, which looks very much like anticipating an apostolic New Testament.

3. A New Testament (as it was called from the second century) actually emerged, as a collection of more or less occasional writings which all assume authority as authentic

communication of God's once-for-all revelation in Christ, and whose authors all identify themselves either by name or by relationship (thus, the author of Hebrews, anonymous to us, is a well-known colleague of Timothy [Heb. 13:23]). Theories of pseudonymous authorship of New Testament books (what was once called forgery) have been diligently explored over many years; here I can only say that none known to me convinces me, and I see strong external grounds in every case for concluding that each book is by the person whose name it bears, quite apart from the evidence of its own internal quality.

4. A number of spurious books ascribed to apostolic authors exist for comparison with our New Testament, and the drop in intellectual, moral, and spiritual calibre is very marked, as are the theological lapses into worlds of commonplace fantasy and magic. In the light of this comparison, there is no reason to think that anything unauthentic crept into the New Testament, or that anything available by a genuine apostolic writer was negligently left out.

5. The Church corporately testifies that the New Testament evidences itself to be the Word of God in a way that no other literature save the Old Testament does. As Jewish guards said of Jesus, 'No-one ever spoke the way this man does' (Jn. 7:46), so God's people down the generations say of the New Testament, 'Never did writing make such an impact on heart and mind and conscience, communicating God, giving knowledge of oneself before God, mediating fellowship with Christ and renewing disordered lives.' Thus has the New Testament evidenced itself through the Spirit to be the Word of God; thus it does still.

The action of making us aware of the unique divine quality of biblical books, the divinity which is the source of the power and authority with which we find them addressing us, is the so-called 'inner witness of the Holy Spirit' in relation to Scripture. This 'inner witness' is not a particular experience or feeling, nor is it a private revelation; it is another name for that enlightenment of our sinful hearts whereby we come to recognize and receive divine realities for what they are –

Jesus Christ as our divine Saviour, Lord and Friend, and Holy Scripture as God's Word to us.[16]

The Church's corporate witness to the divinity of the New Testament is not invalidated by individual oddities like Luther's belief that the 'strawy' epistle of James had no place in the canon since (as he thought, though Lutherans generally, from his lieutenant Melanchthon on, have known better) it contradicts Paul on the point of justification by faith only, without works. Were Paul and James really at odds, Luther's attitude would be defensible, for the inspiring Spirit of God does not contradict Himself; but in fact they differ only in their use of words, while agreeing in substance.[17] And though Luther's view that they were at odds was a scholar's opinion, honestly held, knowledge that he was virtually alone in it should surely have given him pause. Who was Luther to challenge a book which down the centuries had imposed itself on, and been accepted by, the whole Church as part of the New Testament canon? Equally, who am I, and who are you, to do likewise? Surely it will be humbler and wiser to suppose that any present inability on your part or mine to recognize the Word of God in a particular canonical book, or to square what it seems to say with other biblical teaching, reflects a defect in us rather than in it; particularly when (as is invariably the case) learned and devout men can offer a possible, and usually a convincing, resolution of the problem that puzzles us.

So the answer to our question is that the Christian must ask himself, not whether he has reason enough to accept the Church's canon, but whether he has reason enough not to. In reality, he never has.

We need to be clear that the continuing controversies between 'Reformed' and 'Catholic' Christians over such matters as the priesthood of the clergy, the apostolic succession, the authority of the episcopate, the infallibility of the pope, transubstantiation and the 'real presence', the mass-sacrifice, purgatory, indulgences, mariolatry, and the nature and number of the sacraments, cannot in principle be settled until both sides agree that the appeal to Scripture, interpreted in terms of itself – in this sense, *sola Scriptura*, Scripture *alone* – is final.[18]

CHAPTER SIX

GOD'S WORD HEARD

God has spoken, says the Bible; and godliness means *hearing His word*. 'Hearing' in this phrase means more, of course, than just being within earshot while the message of God is read aloud or recited or explained. 'Hear', in its full biblical sense, implies attention, assent, and application to oneself of the things learned; it means listening with a firm purpose to obey, and then doing as God's Word proves to require. It is in this sense that we use the verb throughout this chapter.

What does it mean to hear God's Word? According to Hebrews, it means, quite concretely, receiving and responding to God's propositional Word (that is, His message) which He has spoken to us from heaven through the lips of His personal Word (that is, His Son), also through the utterances of prophets and apostles, concerning the 'great salvation' which the Son of God won for us by the shedding of His blood for our sins (see Heb. 1:1f., 2:3, 12:25, etc.). God's personal Word appears as the central subject of His propositional Word, both when spoken and as written. What Jesus said of the Scriptures of the Old Testament – 'These are the scriptures that testify about me'(Jn. 5:39) – can be said of both Testaments with equal truth. To hear 'God's Word written', therefore, means, in the last analysis, doing as God commanded at the transfiguration, when He said, 'This is my Son, whom I love. Listen to *him*!' (Mk. 9:7); which in its turn means, not just accepting Jesus' moral teaching, but receiving Him as one's living Saviour, relying on His shed blood for the pardon of one's sins, and living henceforth as His bondslave – one of those who 'follow the Lamb wherever he goes' (Rev. 14:4). The homilist reminds us that the living Christ 'speaketh presently unto us in the Holy Scriptures' (*The Homilies*, p. 370f.), and godliness means responding directly to His appeal in repentance, and faith, and discipleship. 'I heard the voice of Jesus say, "Come unto me and rest" . . . I came to Jesus . . .' Nobody who is a stranger to godliness, in this fundamental Christian sense, can be held to have heard God's Word as yet.

Three aspects of the life of godliness, viewed as a life of hearing God's word, call for particular mention.

PROMISE

Firstly, it is a life of *faith in God's promises*. Faith in the Bible is not, as existentialists make out, a leap in the dark, but rather a step in the light, whereby (to extend the metaphor) one puts one's whole weight on the firm ground of God's unshakeable promises. Paul points to Abraham as the great exemplar of faith because, when God promised him, as a childless old man of seventy-five, a host of descendants, he believed the promise, and went on believing it through thick and thin, till it began to be fulfilled in the birth of Isaac, no less than a quarter of a century later. 'Without weakening in his faith, he faced the fact that his body was as good as dead – since he was about a hundred years old – and that Sarah's womb was also dead. Yet he did not waver through unbelief regarding the promise of God, but was strengthened in his faith and gave glory to God, being fully persuaded that God had power to do what he had promised. This is why "it was credited to him as right-eousness."' (Rom. 4:19-22, alluding to the recorded witness to Abraham's justification in Gen. 15:6). Paul's immediate point is that the faith which justifies us is like that – a trust in God on the basis of His incredible-sounding assurance that He gave His Son to die, and then raised Him from death, for the express purpose of putting away our sins (verses 23f.). But this is not the only connection in which Paul's analysis of faith applies. The truth is that all faith, at every stage in our Christian pilgrimage, is essentially a resting upon God's promise. It has the nature of assurance, because it relies on God's assurances. This comes out very clearly in Hebrews 11, where faith ('being sure of what we hope for and certain of what we do not see' [verse 1]) is depicted throughout as a spirit of obedience to God's commands on the basis of trust in His promises, both general (the promise of reward [verse 6]) and particular (such as the promise of a child to Sarah, who 'considered him faithful who had made the promise' [verse 11]).

The heart of the life of faith is in fact the recognition that all the promises which God is recorded as having made to His people in the past are still in principle (not always, of course, in detail, because of differing circumstances) extended to each individual Christian in the present. Faith, we may venture to say, rests upon the theology of the promise-box. This appears from Hebrews 13:5f., where the writer teaches his readers to take to themselves God's promise to Joshua, 'I will never leave you nor forsake you' (Josh. 1:5), as a basis for their own confidence and contentment in face of opposition. The true wellspring of the Christian's peace, joy, hope, and strength to endure, lies in his being able to say, with Isaac Watts,

> Engraved as in eternal brass
>   The mighty promise shines;
> Nor can the powers of darkness raze
>   Those everlasting lines.
>
> His very word of grace is strong
>   As that which built the skies;
> The voice that rolls the stars along
>   Speaks all the promises.
>
> My hiding-place, my refuge, tower,
>   And shield, art Thou, O Lord;
> I firmly anchor all my hopes
>   On thy unerring Word.

The comfort of knowing that every one of God's 'very great and precious promises' (II Pet. 1:4) in Holy Scripture is 'yes' in Christ for me (cf. II Cor. 1:20) is as unspeakable as is the misery of not knowing this in times of hardship, loneliness,

and depression. But such is the state to which those who deny
the biblical doctrine of inspiration sentence themselves; for if
we cannot be sure that what Scripture says, God says, we
cannot be sure that He has actually made any of the promises
which Scripture ascribes to Him. (Indeed if we deny that revelation is propositional, we make it quite certain that He has
not. A God who uses no words cannot make any promises.)

We can now see why, as a matter of observable fact,
'critical' views of the Bible have always impoverished the
life of faith, and why so many of those who hold such
views today either water faith down to mere morality in a
context of vague optimism, or else jazz it up into a tortured
existentialist leap in the dark (or, indeed, like Robinson in
Honest to God, do both together). In the nature of the case,
it could hardly be otherwise. But this is neither the Christian
nor the Anglican way. The Prayer Book points us insistently
to God's promises as the foundation for faith and hope. The
collects for Trinity VI, XI, and XIII sum up the Christian
hope in the phrase 'thy *promises*'. The Catechism requires of
adult candidates for baptism 'faith, whereby they steadfastly
believe *the promises of God* made to them in that sacrament'
(a thought unhappily missing from the Revised Catechism of
1961). One of the hinges on which the infant baptism service
turns is the belief that 'our Lord Jesus Christ hath *promised*
in his Gospel to grant (the child) all these things (saving
gifts and graces) that ye have prayed for'. This emphasis is
specially strong in connection with forgiveness. 'Restore thou
them that are penitent; According to thy *promises* declared
unto mankind in Christ Jesu our Lord' (General Confession,
Morning and Evening Prayer). 'Almighty God ... who ...
hath *promised* forgiveness ... have mercy upon you ...'
(Absolution, holy communion service). And the 'comfortable words' are simply divine promises and assurances, set
forth as a basis for confidence that there is mercy even for
us. Christians today need urgently to recover this Anglican
awareness that the promises of God are the ground of faith;
for where professed Christians are not living in the joy of the
knowledge that all God's promises are theirs, the truth is that
God's Word is not being heard.

LAW

Secondly, godliness involves *obedience to God's laws*. The
Anglican view of the Bible is that it is a supremely practical
book, not only leading us to know God through meeting Jesus
Christ, but also giving us rules and maxims for bringing the
whole of our life into line with God's will. In 1540, in his
Preface to that epoch-making book, the Great Bible, ordered
to be set up for public reading in every church in the country,
Archbishop Cranmer wrote: 'In the Scriptures be the fat
pastures of the soul; therein is no venomous meat, no un-
wholesome thing; they be the very dainty and pure feeding.
He that is ignorant, shall find there what he should learn
. . . Herein may princes learn how to govern their subjects;
subjects obedience . . . to their princes: husbands, how they
should behave them unto their wives; how to educate their
children . . .: and contrary the wives, children, and servants
may know their duty to their husbands, parents, and masters.
Here may all manner of persons, men, women, young, old,
learned, unlearned, rich, poor, priests, laymen, lords, ladies,
officers, tenants, and mean men, virgins, wives, widows,
lawyers, merchants, artificers, husbandmen, and all manner
of persons, of what estate or condition soever they be, may in
this book learn all things what they ought to believe, what they
ought to do, and what they should not do, as well concerning
Almighty God, as also concerning themselves and all other.'[1]
The Bible is as much a rule for life as it is a rule of faith.

But it is important to be clear as to what sort of rule for
life it is. Its moral teaching is not a code of isolated externals,
a Pharisaic formalism, but a connected series of principles
and ideals, deriving directly from the revealed nature of God
and His purpose for mankind, and calling for right motives
as well as right types of action. The biblical law of God
requires us to be persons of a certain kind, as well as to
do things of a certain kind; and the biblical concept of *love*
embraces both sides of the ideal. So opposing love to law, as
some do, is as perverse as opposing a woman's fondness for
her husband to her efforts to provide the things she knows
he likes. So far from being opposed, love and law belong

inseparably together. Law is needed as love's eyes; love is needed as law's heartbeat. Law without love is Pharisaism; love without law is antinomianism; both are aberrations. Our Lord showed the connection between love and law when He said: 'If you love me, you will obey what I command . . . whoever has my commands and obeys them, he is the one who loves me' (Jn. 14:15, 21). John put it even more succinctly: 'love means following the commands of God' (II Jn. 6, N.E.B.). And where Christians do not constantly expose their lives to the detailed 'rebuking, correcting and training in righteousness' of Holy Scripture (II Tim. 3:16), the truth is that God's Word is not being heard.

TRUTH

Thirdly, genuine godliness is always marked by *delight in God's truth*. Psalm 119 makes this abundantly plain. The psalmist loves God's law, rejoices to know God's mind, and holds fast, at whatever cost to himself, the truths that God has taught him. His delight in God is, among other things, a delight in God's Word. Elsewhere in Scripture, God's Word is pictured, not only as food, because it nourishes and promotes growth (I Cor. 3:2; Heb. 5:12ff.; cf. I Pet. 2:2), but also as honey, by reason of its sweetness (Ps. 19:10, 119:103; cf. Ezek. 3:3; Rev. 10:9f.). One fears that many in our churches today are strangers to this sense of the sweetness of God's truth, as they are evidently strangers to the love of the Bible which it evokes, and to the sense of duty to keep God's truth inviolate, come what may, which found expression in the firmness of our Reformers against the pope and the mass – a firmness which under Mary led many to martyrdom. Tolerance of differences on secondary doctrinal questions is doubtless an Anglican virtue, but the all-round doctrinal indifferentism which we meet so often today is a travesty of the Anglican ideal. The Anglicanism of the 1662 Prayer Book, with its hundred-verses-a-day lectionary, its monthly passage through the Psalter, its Bible-crammed daily services, and its high valuation of expository preaching (witness the ordinal, and the collects for Advent III and St. Peter's day), is a Bible-reading, Bible-loving, Bible-believing faith. Today, however, Anglicans devote their zeal to maintaining a state of doctrinal laxity rather than a confession of biblical truth. The Thirty-Nine Articles are constantly deprecated in those Anglican churches that still retain them, and clerical subscription to them is nowadays largely emptied of meaning. The idea that Anglican unity is 'institutional' and 'cultic' rather than confessional is hailed as a new revelation, and all thought of doctrinal discipline in Anglican churches is scouted. What a lapse this is from the Anglicanism of Cranmer, Jewel, Hooper, and Hooker (and, for that matter, of Hammond, Pearson, Beveridge, and Thorndike too!). Where biblical teaching is not revered as a transcript of God's mind, and churchmen show little sign of being ready to '*love* the truth' (II Thess. 2:10), so as to dwell on it, and prize it, and study to keep it intact (cf. II Tim. 1:13f.), and where vital gospel doctrines are allowed to be obscured in the interests of a hollow pleasantness – the thing that Paul would not let happen in Galatia and Colossae – then the truth is that God's Word is not being heard.

THE HOLY SPIRIT

But how, we ask, does God's Word actually come to be heard? In the first place, it will certainly not be heard where the Bible is not preached, studied, or read. The first need is to give the Bible its rightful place in personal and church life. But whether, even then, God's Word will be heard depends on yet a further factor: namely, our openness to the work of the Holy Spirit.

It is the promised privilege of all Christians, we are told, to be 'taught by God' (Jn. 6:45, citing Is. 54:13), and it is the Spirit of God who teaches them. The Spirit who taught all things to the apostles (Jn. 14:26, 16:13f.; I Cor. 2:10, 13) is the 'anointing' that teaches all Christ's people (I Jn. 2:27). He teaches us not by fresh disclosures of hitherto unknown truth, like those whereby the apostles were taught, but by enabling us, who, being fallen, are by nature wholly insensitive and unresponsive to God and the things of God, to acknowledge the reality, recognize the divinity, and bow to the authority, of divine facts and truths set before us, and to see how they bear on our lives. Historically, theologians have called this work illumination, or enlightenment, or the inner witness of the Spirit. It was to this work that our Lord referred when He said that the Spirit's task would be to *convict* (Jn. 16:8). By it, the Spirit authenticates the prophetic and apostolic word to our consciences as being, in truth, what it claims to be, God's message, just as He authenticates Jesus Christ to us as being, in truth, what He claimed to be, God's Son and our Saviour. The Spirit brings us to acknowledge the divinity claimed by, and for, Christ on the one hand, and the Scriptures on the other, as being, in truth, self-evidencing; thus He leads us to bow to the conjoint authority of both. He further enables us to grasp what both are saying to us, and works in our minds and hearts to apply the divine instruction effectively, and make us respond. It was through the Spirit's work that the Thessalonians, having 'received the word of God, which you heard from us [Paul] . . . accepted it not as the word of men, but as it actually is, the word of God'. It was also in virtue of the Spirit's action that Paul could speak of his message as a word which 'is at work in you who believe' (I Thess. 2:13).

But are we open to this working of the Spirit? As long as we approach the Scriptures with detachment, concerned only to appreciate them historically, or aesthetically, and as long as we treat them as a merely human record, we scarcely are. We are only open to the Spirit's ministry so far as we are willing, as it were, to step into the Bible, to take our stand alongside the people to whom God spoke – Abraham listening to God in Ur, Moses listening to God at Sinai, the Israelites listening to God's word from the lips of Moses and the prophets, the Jews listening to Jesus, the Romans and Corinthians and Timothy listening to Paul, and so on – and, in terms of our earlier illustration, to share joint tutorials with them, noting what God said to them and then seeking to see, in the light of that, what He would say to us. Such willingness is in most of us very limited; we are prejudiced, lazy, and unprepared for the exercise of spirit and conscience that it involves. But greater willingness and increased receptiveness are themselves the Spirit's gifts. Therefore we must use the prayer, 'teach me your decrees' (Ps. 119:12, and seven times more in this Psalm), as a plea, not only for teaching but also for teachableness; for without the latter we shall never have the former.

FINDING THE WORD OF THE LORD

We began this book by bringing into focus a problem, the reality of which seems undeniable – namely, that for all the intense biblical study and detailed biblical knowledge of our day, our churches suffer from a widespread 'famine of hearing the words of the Lord'. We have tried to see how this came about, and to outline as simply as we could the way of approach to the Bible which we believe to be both right in itself, and authentically Anglican, and which, if followed, will lead us to the place where God's Word is effectively heard once more. Readers of this book, who, like its writer, are children of an age that is heavily conditioned against the 'old paths' will feel that this approach raises problems. It is no part of our concern to deny this; we would only invite our readers to consider, in the light of what we have said, whether alternative approaches do not raise greater problems still. In a book of this brevity it is not possible to consider many of the problems of which one would have to take note in a treatise, any more than it is possible to deal with the hundred and one questions – exegetical, historical, moral, scientific – that arise when one actually gets down to studying and meditating on the biblical text in the light of the principles stated. Nor, perhaps, would it have been desirable to do so in any case. For this book is offered, not as a treatise, but simply as a tract – a mental and spiritual preparation and, we hope, incentive to the venture of studying the Bible for oneself in the waiting, expectant, God-seeking, God-fearing spirit of Samuel in the temple – 'Speak, for your servant is listening' (I Sam. 3:10). If we allow our study of the Bible to wait upon our finding solutions to every problem that its contents raise, we shall never get started at all. All Bible students carry around with them all their lives a quiverful of unsolved problems, as well as their quota of God-taught certainties. It is idle to expect to find the answer to everything while we are in this world. What matters is that, problems notwithstanding, we should all actually be engaged in searching the Scriptures by the light of right principles and a right method, and so daily learning of God about our sin, and about His Son.

The feeling is sometimes voiced that the sheer quantity of technical information about the Bible which scholars possess today makes Bible study harder for laymen than it used to be, by giving them so much more to master. But the assumption that one cannot study the Bible effectively without a mass of technical theological equipment is false. If the questions one brings to Scripture are such as these – 'What does this tell me about God? about myself? about my Saviour? How does this fit in with the rest of what I know of the Bible? If this is what God said to so-and-so then, what is His word to me here and now? If this is how God dealt with so-and-so in his situation, how would He deal with me in mine?' – and if one pays attention to the context and flow of thought within each book as one reads it, especially if one uses a Bible with good marginal references, God the Spirit will see to it that, lay person no less than theologian, one will learn what one needs to know.

What *does* make Bible study harder for laypeople nowadays than it used to be is the widespread breakdown of the great evangelical tradition of large-scale expository preaching Sunday by Sunday from our pulpits. The New Testament pattern is that public preaching of God's Word provides, so to speak, the main meals, and constitutes the chief means of grace, and one's own personal meditations on biblical truth should come in as ancillary to this, having the nature of a series of supplementary snacks – necessary, indeed, in their place, but never intended to stand alone as a complete diet. There is something deeply unnatural and unsatisfactory in a situation where the people of God have to rely entirely on personal Bible study for their spiritual nourishment, due to lack of effective expository preaching in public worship. But this is a different issue, which we cannot pursue here.

Let it be clear, once more, that we are not belittling technical biblical scholarship. Our only point is that it is not to biblical experts alone that the Holy Spirit vouchsafes His teaching, and that the psalmist's description of the law of the Lord as 'making wise the simple' (Ps. 19:7) still holds good.

At the 1958 Lambeth Conference, the first committee report dealt with 'The Holy Bible: its Authority and Message'.[2] Despite some unhappy features (its denial of the sufficiency of Scripture, noted above,[3] and of biblical inerrancy, and the inadequacy of its treatment of the biblical thought of God as speaking),[4] it contained much that was excellent, and laid specially welcome emphasis on the importance of biblical exposition in the pulpit and the reading of the Bible personally and in the home. In this, of course, it simply reaffirmed foundation-principles of Reformed Anglicanism. The Conference as a whole endorsed the report with a series of resolutions, including a call to 'all Church people to re-establish the habit of Bible-reading at home',[5] and a summons to 'the Churches of the Anglican Communion to engage in a special effort during the next ten years to extend the scope and deepen the quality of personal and corporate study of the Bible'.[6] The Encyclical Letter spoke in this connection of the clergyman's duty to work at his preaching in order to make the Bible 'come alive' to his hearers, and of 'the duty of the laity to bring to the hearing of the Bible an expectant heart, and to learn again the art of private Bible study and meditation'.[7] Admirable words – but it seems that neither in the decade following 1958 nor since has any serious response to them been made. Anglicans in the Western world generally, along with many other contemporary Christians, remain largely strangers to the Bible.

> God therefore, for His mercies' sake, vouchsafe to purify our minds through faith in His Son Jesus Christ, and to instil the heavenly drops of His grace into our hard stony hearts, to supple the same, that we be not contemners and deriders of His infallible Word; but that with all humbleness of mind and Christian reverence, we may endeavour ourselves to hear and to read His sacred Scriptures, and inwardly so to digest them, as shall be to the comfort of our

souls, and sanctification of His holy name: to whom with the Son and the Holy Ghost, three Persons and one living God, be all laud, honour, and praise, for ever and ever. Amen (*The Homilies*, p. 383).

O Almighty God, who by thy Son Jesus Christ didst give to Thy apostle Saint Peter many excellent gifts, and commandedst him earnestly to feed Thy flock; Make, we beseech Thee, all bishops and pastors diligently to preach Thy holy Word, and the people obediently to follow the same, that they may receive the crown of everlasting glory; through Jesus Christ our Lord. Amen (collect for Saint Peter's day).

Blessed Lord, who hast caused all holy Scriptures to be written for our learning; Grant that we may in such wise hear them, read, mark, learn, and inwardly digest them, that by patience, and comfort of Thy holy Word, we may embrace, and ever hold fast the blessed hope of everlasting life, which Thou has given us in our Saviour Jesus Christ. Amen (collect for Advent II).

Today if ye will hear his voice, harden not your hearts: as in the provocation, and as in the day of temptation in the wilderness;

When your fathers tempted Me: proved Me, and saw My works.

Forty years long was I grieved with this generation, and said: It is a people that do err in their hearts, for they have not known My ways.

Unto whom I sware in my wrath: that they should not enter into My rest (Ps. 95:7-11, Prayer Book version).

NOTES

FOREWORD

1 James Barr: *Fundamentalism* (London, 1977, 2nd ed.1987); see also his *Escaping from Fundamentalism* (London, 1984).

CHAPTER 2

1 *The Lambeth Conference 1958* (London, 1958), 1, 33.
2 *Confessions*, xiii, 29.
3 C. Hodge: op. cit. (London, 1873), Vol. I, p. 162.
4 Wellhausen's theory has been damagingly criticized by conservative scholars such as W. H. Green: *The Higher Criticism of the Pentateuch* (New York, 1895); J. Orr: *The Problem of the Old Testament* (London, 1900); R. D. Wilson: A *Scientific Investigation of the Old Testament* (New York, 1926); O. T. Allis: *The Five Books of Moses* (Philadelphia, 1943); G. Ch. Aalders: A *Short Introduction to the Pentateuch* (London, 1949); E. J. Young: *Introduction to the Old Testament* (Grand Rapids, 1949; London, 1954); R. K. Harrison: *Introduction to the Old Testament* (London, 1970). Roman Catholic scholars often reject it, as does the modern Scandinavian school, but it keeps the field in most Protestant circles because no alternative theory seems to account for so many of the phenomena so neatly. It is admitted, however, by most scholars today that its truth is an open question, not a closed one, as was once thought. See D. A. Hubbard in *The New Bible Dictionary*, ed. J. D. Douglas, N. Hillyer, F. F. Bruce, J. I. Packer, R. V. G. Tasker, D. J. Wiseman, D. Guthrie, A. R. Millard (Leicester, 1980), s.v. 'Pentateuch'.
5 J. Baillie: op. cit. (London, 1956), p. 109.
6 D. E. Nineham: *The Church's Use of the Bible Past and*

Present (London, 1963), p. 162, referring to *The Revised Catechism* (1961). Nineham seems to think that human nature so changes from one age and cultural milieu to another that modern Westerners simply cannot grasp what the New Testament in particular was written to convey; see *The Use and Abuse of The Bible* (London, 1976), and my comments on Nineham's view in 'Infallible Scripture and the Role of Hermeneutics': *Scripture and Truth*, ed. D. A. Carson and J. B. Woodbridge (Leicester, 1983), pp. 331f.

7 The accusation, often made, that evangelical (and, for that matter, most pre-Vatican II Roman Catholic) biblical scholarship does just this is misguided. What it does, rather, is to face frankly the problems about the Bible which scientific and historical enquiry raises, and then to live with them until such time as satisfying solutions appear, on the principle, stated by Augustine, that 'if we cannot reconcile such a contradiction (*sc.*, between the apparent results of secular study on the one hand and Bible study on the other) we are to suspend judgment, not doubting either the Holy Scripture or the results of human observation and reasoning, but believing that it is possible, given sufficient knowledge and understanding, to reconcile the apparent contradiction.'

8 *The Homilies*, ed. G. E. Corrie (Cambridge, 1850), pp. 370, 378, 383.

CHAPTER 3

1 *Westminster Theological Journal*, May 1960 (XXII, ii), pp. 127f.

2 *Our Faith* (London, 1936; 1949 edn.) p. 12.

3 Calvin: *Institutes of the Christian Religion*, II,ii, 18.

4 Among good surveys of non-Christian faiths are J. N. D. Anderson (ed.): *The World's Religions* (2nd. ed., London, 1951); H. D. Lewis and R. L. Slater: *The Study of Religions* (London, Pelican Books, 1969); G. Parrinder: *The World's Living Religions* (London, Pan Piper, 1964); N. Smart: *The Religious Experience of Mankind* (London, 1969). For model approaches to them, see J. N. D. Anderson: *Christianity and Comparative Religion* (London, 1970); A. K. Cragg: *Christian and Other Religions* (Oxford, 1977); S. C. Neill: *Crises of Belief* (London, 1984). Currently in progress is

a debate, prompted by the 'anonymous Christians' idea of
the late Karl Rahner and the universalist speculations of
John Hick, as to whether the world's major religions really
converge and whether there is salvation in Christ for adult
adherents of non-Christian faiths. For an orientation see H. A.
Netland:*Dissonant Voices* (Leicester, 1991); J. Sanders: *No
Other Name* (Grand Rapids, 1992).

5 The statement in the text reproduces Barth's own: see *Church
Dogmatics*, I.2.528f. (Edinburgh, 1956). It should be said,
however, that Barth's method throughout the 7,000-odd pages
of the *Church Dogmatics* is to establish each point by his
own characteristic biblical exegesis, and at no point does he
dissent from what he finds in the text.

CHAPTER 4

1 This emphasis, characteristic of the British 'biblical theology'
movement and the continental '*Heilsgeschichte*' theologians
(cf., on the latter, Alan Richardson: *The Bible in the Age of
Science* [London, 1961], pp. 122ff.), found typical expression
in such books as Gabriel Hebert: *The Bible from Within*
(Oxford, 1950); William Neil: *The Rediscovery of the Bible*
(London, 1954); Oscar Cullmann: *Christ and Time* (Eng. tr.,
London, 1951); G. E. Wright: *God Who Acts* (London, 1952);
and in the Committee Report on the Holy Bible at the 1958
Lambeth Conference *(The Lambeth Conference 1958*, 2, 2ff.,
especially pp. 9-12). B. S. Childs: *Biblical Theology in Crisis*
(Philadelphia, 1970), tells how, for alleged exegetical, critical,
linguistic and hermeneutical naiveties, biblical theology went
under a cloud in the 1960s. It has re-emerged in strength,
however, in such work as William Dumbrell: *Covenant
and Creation* (Nashville, 1986).

2 The London-Edinburgh express named the 'Flying Scotsman'
dates back to the mid-nineteenth century. The steam
locomotive named 'Flying Scotsman' (an A3 Pacific) was built
in 1923, and has been preserved.

3 See Temple: *Nature, Man and God* (London, 1934), Lecture
xii, and his essay in *Revelation*, ed. D. M. Baillie and H.
Martin (London, 1937); Hodgson: *The Doctrine of the
Trinity* (London, 1943), Lecture i.

4 *Nature, Man and God*, p. 317.

5 Thus, for instance, George Every wrote of Herbert Kelly:
   'In his own reflections on the Old Testament Father Kelly
   had a way of going directly to the event, without even
   noticing the interpretation given by the prophet or the
   prophetic historian' (H. Kelly: *The Gospel of God* [London,
   1959 ed.], p. 34). In this Kelly was showing himself less
   a prophet to our time than a child of it. D. B. Knox
   comments: 'It will be seen that if revelation is in the event
   rather than in the interpretation, revelation becomes like
   a nose of wax to be reshaped according to every man's
   whim' ('Propositional Revelation the Only Revelation':
   Reformed Theological Review, February 1960 [XIX, 1],
   p. 5).

6 Hammond was England's premier batsman in the thirties.
   I recall a moment of fearful ecstasy in Gloucester when
   he lifted a beautiful six over the square-leg boundary. I
   was watching there and I thought the ball was going to hit
   me.

7 *The Authority of the Bible* (London, 1960 ed.), p. 83.

8 See further my *'Fundamentalism' and the Word of God*
   (London, 1958); 'Revelation and Inspiration': *The New
   Bible Commentary* (2nd ed., London, 1954), pp. 21ff.;
   'Revelation': *The New Bible Dictionary* (London,
   1962).

9 Commentary on *Hebrews*, ad loc. (London, 1840 ed., Vol. II,
   pp. 19, 20).

10 *Institutes*, I, vi. 2.

CHAPTER 5

1 See pp.35-43 above.

2 Modern Roman Catholic achievement in this field
   may be gauged by two books which, apart from their
   inevitable weaknesses regarding justification and the
   Church, are in the main very fine: C. Charlier: *The
   Christian Approach to the Bible* (Eng. tr., London,
   1958); L. Bouyer: *The Meaning of Sacred Scripture*
   (Eng. tr., Indiana and London, 1960). *The Jerome Bible*

Commentary, ed. R. E. Brown, J. A. Fitzmyer and R. E. Murphy (Englewood Cliffs, 1968), was and remains a landmark of Roman Catholic scholarship. It must be noted, however, that the Constitution on Revelation of the Second Vatican Council has opened the floodgates for much sceptical biblical criticism among Roman Catholics. Section 11 of the Constitution says: 'the books of Scripture must be acknowledged as teaching firmly, faithfully and without error that truth which God wanted put in the sacred writings for the sake of our salvation'. Leading Roman Catholic theologians expound this as meaning that only truths necessary to salvation are guaranteed inerrant, and these (some of the theologians add), are few. Thus Roman Catholics are now joining Protestants in giving up the axiom that what Scripture says, God says. See J. I. Packer, 'Encountering Present-day Views of Scripture': *The Foundation of Biblical Authority*, ed. James M. Boice (Grand Rapids, 1978), pp. 61ff., especially pp. 74-76; John W. Montgomery, 'The Approach of New Shape Roman Catholicism to Scriptural Inerrancy: a Case Study': *God's Inerrant Word*, ed. John W. Montgomery (Minneapolis, 1974) pp. 263ff.; David F. Wells: *Revolution in Rome* (London 1973), pp. 26ff.

3   J. A. T. Robinson: *Honest to God*, p. 25; text of letter in ed. D. A. Edwards: *The Honest to God Debate* (London, 1963), pp. 138f.

4   B. B. Warfield: *The Inspiration and Authority of the Bible* (London, 1951), p. 155.

5   See, for proof of this, and discussion of the passages in Christ's teaching which some take as showing His rejection of Old Testament authority, J. W. Wenham: *Our Lord's View of the Old Testament* (London, 1953), especially pp. 28ff.; *Christ and the Bible* (London, 1972), ch. 1; 'Christ's View of Scripture': *Inerrancy*, ed. N. L. Geisler (Grand Rapids, 1980); R. V. G. Tasker: *Our Lord's Use of the Old Testament* (London, 1953); Chapter II of *The Old Testament in the New Testament*: (2nd. ed., London, 1954); N. B. Stonehouse: *The Witness of Matthew and Mark to Christ* (Philadelphia, 1944); J. I. Packer: *Our Lord's Understanding of the Law of God* (London, 1962).

6 See N. Geldenhuys: *Supreme Authority* (London, 1953), especially pp. 45ff.

7 J. D. Wood: *The Interpretation of the Bible* (London, 1958), pp. 1f.

8 A. Kuyper observes that the standpoint of the inspired poets who wrote these Psalms was that of ultimate spiritual reality, where distinctions are absolute and 'everything that sides with God lives and has our love, and everything that chooses eternally against God bears the mark of death and rouses our hatred'. This is the standpoint that we shall all occupy in heaven, though we cannot consistently attain to it here. Seeing things from this standpoint, says Kuyper, 'the rule, "Do not I hate them, O Lord, that hate thee?" becomes the only applicable standard, and whatever departs from this rule, falls short of love for God . . . [the imprecations] are solemnly true and holy when you take your stand in the absolute palingenesis [i.e., the order of new creation, eschatologically viewed], where God's honour is the keynote of the harmony of the human heart' (*Principles of Sacred Theology* [Grand Rapids, 1954], p. 524). It will help us progressively to appropriate these Psalms and enter into their outlook if we learn to use them as prayers against Satan and his hosts, and against our own besetting sins. Cf. C. S. Lewis: *Reflections on the Psalms* (London, 1961 ed.), pp. 113f.

9 See the phrase quoted from *The Homilies* ('An Information . . .') on p. 36 above. Archbishop Cranmer and Bishops Ridley and Jewel also used the word. John Wycliffe in the fourteenth century called the Bible *infallibilis regula fidei* (an infallible rule of faith).

10 Calvin, *Institutes of the Christian Religion*, I, vii, 5.

11 The *New Bible Dictionary* (Leicester and Grand Rapids, 1980), the one-volume *New Bible Commentary Revised* (London and Grand Rapids, 1970), the *Zondervan Pictorial Encyclopaedia of the Bible* (Grand Rapids, 1975), the Tyndale and New International commentary series, D. Guthrie: *New Testament Introduction* (London, 1970), and J. W. Wenham: *Christ and the Bible* and *The Goodness of God* (London, 1972, 1974) and Gleason Archer: *Encyclopaedia of Bible Difficulties* (Grand Rapids, 1982), are among the most helpful scholarly sources of light on challenged parts of Scripture.

12 For the first, see pp. 71ff. above.

13 Regrettably, this principle found its way into the Committee
Report on the Bible at the 1958 Lambeth Conference.
'The Anglican Communion appeals to the whole of that
primitive tradition of which the Sacraments, the Creeds,
the Canon of the Bible, and the historic episcopate are
all parts. The New Testament is thus not to be seen in
isolation: the Church preceded it in time, and it was within
the Church, with its Sacraments, Creeds, and Apostolic
Ministry, that the New Testament was canonized' (*The
Lambeth Conference 1958*, 2,4).

14 E. A. Litton: *Introduction to Dogmatic Theology* (London,
1960 ed.), pp. 30f.

15 For more details on the formation of the New Testament
canon, and the principles involved in it, see J. W. Wenham,
op. cit., ch. 6, and Herman N. Ridderbos: 'The Canon of
the New Testament' in *Revelation and the Bible*, ed. C. F.
H. Henry (Grand Rapids and London, 1958), pp. 187ff.; *The
Authority of the New Testament Scriptures* (Philadelphia,
1963); J. N. Birdsall: 'Canon of the New Testament' in
The New Bible Dictionary (1980); Bruce Metzger: *The
Canon of the New Testament* (Oxford, 1987); F. F. Bruce:
The Canon of Scripture (Leicester, 1988). The statement
in Article VI that the books of the New Testament 'as they
are commonly received' are those 'of whose authority was
never any doubt in the Church' is a little too loose to be
quite clear. The meaning apparently is that the authenticity
and authority of these books was never doubted, not by
individual theologians and congregations (the framers of
the Articles were well aware that such a statement, if made,
would be false), but by the catholic visible Church as a
whole. So understood, the statement, so far as the available
evidence goes, would seem to be true.

16 Two statements by John Calvin, who first formulated this
concept of the 'inner witness' (picking up, as so often, hints
dropped by Luther), merit quotation here. 'Enlightened by
him (the Holy Spirit), we no longer believe that Scripture is
from God either on our own judgment or on that of others;
but, in a way that surpasses human judgment, we are made
absolutely certain, just as if we beheld there the majesty of
God himself, that it has come to us by the ministry of men
from God's very mouth.' 'Scripture will ultimately suffice
for a saving knowledge of God only when certainty about

it is founded on the inward persuasion of the Holy Spirit (*Institutes of the Christian Religion*, I. vii. 5, viii. 13).

[17] It is worth showing this. The problem concerns Jas. 2:18-26 as compared with Rom. 3:21-5:21 and Gal. 3, and particularly what is said of Abraham in these passages. The key is to see that (i) to be 'justified' is Paul's technical term for being pardoned and accepted by God, whereas for James it means being vindicated in a claim one has made, or that has been made for one (in this case, evidently, the claim that Abraham was truly in fellowship with God); (ii) 'faith' is for Paul the responsive energy of the regenerate heart, whereas James uses the word as he imagines the person he addresses using it, for orthodox beliefs as such; (iii) 'works', which for Paul signify self-justifying self-effort, signify for James the service of God whereby faith finds appropriate expression: in other words, the same as Paul means when he says '*good* works'. James' subject is not the way of salvation, but the proof of genuineness when one claims a relation to God, and his point is that orthodoxy alone means nothing – which is precisely Paul's point in Rom. 2:17-29.

[18] See on this R. T. Beckwith, G. E. Duffield, and J. I. Packer: *Across the Divide* (Basingstoke, 1978), containing text and exposition of the evangelical Open Letter to the Anglican episcopate about relations with the Roman Catholic and Eastern Churches. The three Anglican-Roman Catholic Agreements, on the Eucharist, the Doctrine of the Ministry, and Authority, all fail at key points to be biblical enough in the sense defined.

CHAPTER 6

[1] Cranmer: *Remains and Letters* (Parker Society: Cambridge, 1846), p. 121.

[2] *The Lambeth Conference 1958*, 2, 1-18.

[3] Ibid. See also Ch5, note 13. Above, p. 116, note 1.

[4] 2, 7.

[5] 1, 33 (Resolution 5).

[6] 1, 34 (Resolution 12).

[7] 1, 19.

THE CHICAGO STATEMENT ON BIBLICAL INERRANCY (1978)

In October 1978 an international conference of nearly 300 theological scholars and church leaders from all Protestant denominations met at Chicago under the auspices of the International Council on Biblical Inerrancy and produced the following statement, to which almost all conference members subscribed, The statement responds to widespread intramural debate among professed evangelical Christians in North America over several years. I shared in drafting it and myself subscribed to it, and reproduce it here by permission. I do so partly because of the weight of representative authority which it carries and partly because of its intrinsic value as an expression of the view of Holy Scripture which this book advocates.

PREFACE

THE STATEMENT

The authority of Scripture is a key issue for the Christian Church in this and every age. Those who profess faith in Jesus Christ as Lord and Saviour are called to show the reality of their discipleship by humbly and faithfully obeying God's written Word. To stray from Scripture in faith or conduct is disloyalty to our Master. Recognition of the total truth and trustworthiness of Holy Scripture is essential to a full grasp and adequate confession of its authority.

The following Statement affirms this inerrancy of Scripture afresh, making clear our understanding of it and warning against its denial. We are persuaded that to deny it is to set aside the witness of Jesus Christ and of the Holy Spirit and to refuse that submission to the claims of God's own Word which marks true Christian faith. We see it as our timely duty to make this affirmation in the face of current lapses from the truth of inerrancy among our fellow Christians and misunderstanding of this doctrine in the world at large.

This Statement consists of three parts: a Summary Statement, Articles of Affirmation and Denial, and an accompanying Exposition. It has been prepared in the course of a three-day consultation in Chicago. Those who have signed the Summary Statement and the Articles wish to affirm their own conviction as to the inerrancy of Scripture and to encourage and challenge one another and all Christians to growing appreciation and understanding of this doctrine. We acknowledge the limitations of a document prepared in a brief, intensive conference and do not propose that this Statement be given credal weight. Yet we rejoice in the deepening of our own convictions through our discussions together, and we pray that the Statement we have signed may be used to the glory of our God toward a new reformation of the Church in its faith, life, and mission.

We offer this Statement in a spirit, not of contention, but of humility and love, which we purpose by God's grace to maintain in any future dialogue arising out of what we have said. We gladly acknowledge that many who deny the inerrancy of Scripture do not display the consequences of this denial in the rest of their belief and behaviour, and we are conscious that we who confess this doctrine often deny it in life by failing to bring our thoughts and deeds, our traditions and habits, into true subjection to the divine Word.

We invite response to this statement from any who see reason to amend its affirmations about Scripture by the light of Scripture itself, under whose infallible authority we stand as we speak. We claim no personal infallibility for the witness we bear, and for any help which enables us to strengthen this testimony to God's Word we shall be grateful.

The Draft Committee

A SHORT STATEMENT

1. God, who is Himself Truth and speaks truth only, has inspired Holy Scripture in order thereby to reveal Himself to lost mankind through Jesus Christ as Creator and Lord, Redeemer and Judge. Holy Scripture is God's witness to Himself.

2. Holy Scripture, being God's own Word, written by men prepared and superintended by His Spirit, is of infallible divine authority in all matters upon which it touches: it is to be believed, as God's instruction, in all that it affirms; obeyed, as God's command, in all that it requires; embraced, as God's pledge, in all that it promises.

3. The Holy Spirit, its divine Author, both authenticates it to us by His inward witness and opens our minds to understand its meaning.

4. Being wholly and verbally God-given, Scripture is without error or fault in all its teaching, no less in what it states about God's acts in creation, about the events of world history, and about its own literary origins under God, than in its witness to God's saving grace in individual lives.

5. The authority of Scripture is inescapably impaired if this total divine inerrancy is in any way limited or disregarded, or made relative to a view of truth contrary to the Bible's own; and such lapses bring serious loss to both the individual and the Church.

ARTICLES OF AFFIRMATION AND DENIAL

Article I.   We affirm that the Holy Scriptures are to be received as the authoritative Word of God.

We deny that the Scriptures receive their authority from the Church, tradition, or any other human source.

Article II.   We affirm that the Scriptures are the supreme written norm by which God binds the conscience, and that the authority of the Church is subordinate to that of Scripture.

We deny that Church creeds, councils, or declarations have authority greater than or equal to the authority of the Bible.

Article III. We affirm that the written Word in its entirety is revelation given by God.

We deny that the Bible is merely a witness to Revelation, or only becomes revelation in encounter, or depends on the responses of men for its validity.

Article IV.   We affirm that God who made mankind in His image has used language as a means of revelation.

We deny that human language is so limited by our creatureliness that it is rendered inadequate as a vehicle for divine revelation. We further deny that the corruption of human culture and language through sin has thwarted God's work of inspiration.

Article V.   We affirm that God's revelation within the Holy Scriptures was progressive.

We deny that later revelation, which may fulfil earlier revelation, ever corrects or contradicts it. We further deny that any normative revelation has been given since the completion of the New Testament writings.

Article VI.   We affirm that the whole of Scripture and all its parts, down to the very words of the original, were given by divine inspiration.

We deny that the inspiration of Scripture can rightly be affirmed of the whole without the parts, or of some parts but not the whole.

Article VII.   We affirm that inspiration was the work in which God by His Spirit, through human writers, gave us His Word. The origin of Scripture is divine. The mode of divine inspiration remains largely a mystery to us.

We deny that inspiration can be reduced to human insight, or to heightened states of consciousness of any kind.

Article VIII.   We affirm that God in His work of inspiration utilized the distinctive personalities and literary styles of the writers whom He had chosen and prepared.

We deny that God, in causing these writers to use the very words that He chose, overrode their personalities.

Article IX.   We affirm that inspiration, though not conferring omniscience, guaranteed true and trustworthy utterance on all matters of which the Biblical authors were moved to speak and write.

We deny that the finitude or fallenness of these writers, by necessity or otherwise, introduced distortion or falsehood into God's Word.

Article X.

We affirm that inspiration, strictly speaking, applies only to the autographic text of Scripture, which in the providence of God can be ascertained from available manuscripts with great accuracy. We further affirm that copies and translations of Scripture are the Word of God to the extent that they faithfully represent the original.

We deny that any essential element of the Christian faith is affected by the absence of the autographs. We further deny that this absence renders the assertion of Biblical inerrancy invalid or irrelevant.

Article XI.

We affirm that Scripture, having been given by divine inspiration, is infallible, so that, far from misleading us, it is true and reliable in all the matters it addresses.

We deny that it is possible for the Bible to be at the same time infallible and errant in its assertions. Infallibility and inerrancy may be distinguished, but not separated.

Article XII.

We affirm that Scripture in its entirety is inerrant, being free from all falsehood, fraud, or deceit.

We deny that Biblical infallibility and inerrancy are limited to spiritual, religious, or redemptive themes, exclusive of assertions in the fields of history and science. We further deny that scientific hypotheses about earth history may properly be used to overturn the teaching of Scripture on creation and the flood.

Article XIII. We affirm the propriety of using inerrancy as a theological term with reference to the complete truthfulness of Scripture.

We deny that it is proper to evaluate Scripture according to standards of truth and error that are alien to its usage or purpose. We further deny that inerrancy is negated by Biblical phenomena such as a lack of modern technical precision, irregularities of grammar or spelling, observational descriptions of nature, the reporting of falsehoods (*e.g.* the lies of Satan), the use of hyperbole and round numbers, the topical arrangement of material, variant selections of material in parallel accounts, or the use of free citations.

Article XIV. We affirm the unity and internal consistency of Scripture.

We deny that alleged errors and discrepancies that have not yet been resolved vitiate the truth claims of the Bible.

Article XV. We affirm that the doctrine of inerrancy is grounded in the teaching of the Bible about inspiration.

We deny that Jesus' teaching about Scripture may be dismissed by appeals to accommodation or to any natural limitation of His humanity.

Article XVI. We affirm that the doctrine of inerrancy has been integral to the Church's faith throughout its history.

We deny that inerrancy is a doctrine invented by scholastic Protestantism, or is a reactionary position postulated in response to negative higher criticism.

Article XVII.

We affirm that the Holy Spirit bears witness to the Scriptures, assuring believers of the truthfulness of God's written Word.

We deny that this witness of the Holy Spirit operates in isolation from or against Scripture.

Article XVIII.

We affirm that the text of Scripture is to be interpreted by grammatico-historical exegesis, taking account of its literary forms and devices, and that Scripture is to interpret Scripture.

We deny the legitimacy of any treatment of the text or quest for sources lying behind it that leads to relativizing, dehistoricizing, or discounting its teaching, or rejecting its claims to authorship.

Article XIX.

We affirm that a confession of the full authority, infallibility, and inerrancy of Scripture is vital to a sound understanding of the whole of the Christian faith. We further affirm that such confession should lead to increasing conformity to the image of Christ.

We deny that such confession is necessary for salvation. However, we further deny that inerrancy can be rejected without grave consequences, both to the individual and to the Church.

EXPOSITION

Our understanding of the doctrine of inerrancy must be set in the context of the broader teachings of the Scripture concerning itself. This exposition gives an account of the outline of doctrine from which our summary statement and articles are drawn.

Creation, Revelation and Inspiration

The Triune God, who formed all things by His creative utterances and governs all things by His Word of decree, made mankind in His own image for a life of communion with Himself, on the model of the eternal fellowship of loving communication within the Godhead. As God's image-bearer, man was to hear God's Word addressed to him and to respond in the joy of adoring obedience. Over and above God's self-disclosure in the created order and the sequence of events within it, human beings from Adam on have received verbal messages from Him, either directly, as stated in Scripture, or indirectly in the form of part or all of Scripture itself.

When Adam fell, the Creator did not abandon mankind to final judgment but promised salvation and began to reveal Himself as Redeemer in a sequence of historical events centring on Abraham's family and culminating in the life, death, resurrection, present heavenly ministry, and promised return of Jesus Christ. Within this frame God has from time to time spoken specific words of judgment and mercy, promise and command, to sinful human beings, so drawing them into a covenant relation of mutual commitment between Him and them in which He blesses them with gifts of grace and they bless Him in responsive adoration. Moses, whom God used as mediator to carry His words to His people at the time of the Exodus, stands at the head of a long line of prophets into whose mouths and writings God put His words for delivery to Israel. God's purpose in this succession of messages was to maintain His covenant by causing His people to know His Name – that is, His nature – and His will both of precept and purpose in the present and for the future. This line of prophetic spokesmen from God came to completion in Jesus Christ, God's incarnate Word, who was Himself a prophet – more than a prophet, but not less – and in the apostles and prophets of the first Christian generation. When God's final and climactic message, His word to the world concerning Jesus Christ, had been spoken and elucidated by those in the apostolic circle, the sequence of revealed messages ceased. Henceforth the Church was to live and know God by what He had already said, and said for all time.

At Sinai God wrote the terms of His covenant on tables of stone, as His enduring witness and for lasting accessibility, and throughout the period of prophetic and apostolic revelation He prompted men to write the messages given to and through them, along with celebratory records of His dealings with His people, plus moral reflections on covenant life and forms of praise and prayer for covenant mercy. The theological reality of inspiration in the producing of Biblical documents corresponds to that of spoken prophecies: although the human writers' personalities were expressed in what they wrote, the words were divinely constituted. Thus, what Scripture says, God says; its authority is His authority, for He is its ultimate Author, having given it through the minds and words of chosen and prepared men who in freedom and faithfulness 'spoke from God as they were carried along by the Holy Spirit' (I Pet. 1:21). Holy Scripture must be acknowledged as the Word of God by virtue of its divine origin.

Authority: Christ and the Bible

Jesus Christ, the Son of God who is the Word made flesh, our Prophet, Priest, and King, is the ultimate Mediator of God's communication to man, as He is of all God's gifts of grace.

The revelation He gave was more than verbal; He revealed the Father by His presence and His deeds as well. Yet His words were crucially important; for He was God, He spoke from the Father, and His words will judge all men at the last day.

As the prophesied Messiah, Jesus Christ is the central theme of Scripture. The Old Testament looked ahead to Him; the New Testament looks back to His first coming and on to His second. Canonical Scripture is the divinely inspired and therefore normative witness to Christ. No hermeneutic, therefore, of which the historical Christ is not the focal point is acceptable. Holy Scripture must be treated as what it essentially is – the witness of the Father to the incarnate Son.

It appears that the Old Testament canon had been fixed by the time of Jesus. The New Testament canon is likewise now closed inasmuch as no new apostolic witness to the historical Christ can now be borne. No new revelation (as distinct from Spirit-given understanding of existing revelation) will be given until Christ comes again. The canon was created in principle by divine inspiration. The Church's part was to discern the canon which God had created, not to devise one of its own.

The word *canon*, signifying a rule or standard, is a pointer to authority, which means the right to rule and control. Authority in Christianity belongs to God in His revelation, which means, on the one hand, Jesus Christ, the living Word, and, on the other hand, Holy Scripture, the written Word. But the authority of Christ and that of Scripture are one. As our Priest, Christ testified that Scripture cannot be broken. As our Priest and King, He devoted His earthly life to fulfilling the law and the prophets, even dying in obedience to the words of Messianic prophecy. Thus, as He saw Scripture attesting Him and His authority, so by His own submission to Scripture He attested its authority. As He bowed to His Father's instruction given in His Bible (our Old Testament), so He requires His disciples to do – not, however, in isolation but in conjunction with the apostolic witness to Himself which He undertook to inspire by His gift of the Holy Spirit. So Christians show themselves faithful servants of their Lord by bowing to the divine instruction given in the prophetic and apostolic writings which together make up our Bible.

By authenticating each other's authority, Christ and Scripture coalesce into a single fount of authority. The Biblically-interpreted Christ and the Christ-centred, Christ-proclaiming Bible are from this standpoint one. As from the fact of inspiration we infer that what Scripture says, God says, so from the revealed relation between Jesus Christ and Scripture we may equally declare that what Scripture says, Christ says.

Infallibility, Inerrancy, Interpretation

Holy Scripture, as the inspired Word of God witnessing authoritatively to Jesus Christ, may properly be called *infallible* and *inerrant*. These negative terms have a special value, for they explicitly safeguard crucial positive truths.

Infallible signifies the quality of neither misleading nor being misled and so safeguards in categorical terms the truth that Holy Scripture is a sure, safe, and reliable rule and guide in all matters.

Similarly, *inerrant* signifies the quality of being free from all falsehood or mistake and so safeguards the truth that Holy Scripture is entirely true and trustworthy in all its assertions.

We affirm that canonical Scripture should always be interpreted on the basis that it is infallible and inerrant. However, in determining what the God-taught writer is asserting in each passage, we must pay the most careful attention to its claims and character as a human production. In inspiration. God utilized the culture and conventions of His penman's milieu, a milieu that God controls in His sovereign providence; it is misinterpretation to imagine otherwise.

So history must be treated as history, poetry as poetry, hyperbole and metaphor as hyperbole and metaphor, generalization and approximation as what they are, and so forth. Differences between literary conventions in Bible times and in ours must also be observed: since, for instance, non-chronological narration and imprecise citation were conventional and acceptable and violated no expectations in those days, we must not regard these things as faults when we find them in Bible writers. When total precision of a particular kind was not expected nor aimed at, it is no error not to have achieved it. Scripture is inerrant, not in the sense of being absolutely precise by modern standards, but in the sense of making good its claims and achieving that measure of focused truth at which its authors aimed.

The truthfulness of Scripture is not negated by the appearance in it of irregularities of grammar or spelling, phenomenal descriptions of nature, reports of false statements (*e.g.* the lies of Satan), or seeming discrepancies between one passage and another. It is not right to set the so-called 'phenomena' of Scripture against the teaching of Scripture about itself. Apparent inconsistencies should not be ignored. Solution of them, where this can be convincingly achieved, will encourage our faith, and where for the present no convincing solution is at hand we shall significantly honour God by trusting His assurance that His Word is true, despite these appearances, and by maintaining our confidence that one day they will be seen to have been illusions.

Inasmuch as all Scripture is the product of a single divine mind, interpretation must stay within the bounds of the analogy of Scripture and eschew hypotheses that would correct one Biblical passage by another, whether in the name of progressive revelation or of the imperfect enlightenment of the inspired writer's mind.

Although Holy Scripture is nowhere culture-bound in the sense that its teaching lacks universal validity, it is sometimes culturally conditioned by the customs and conventional views of a particular period, so that the application of its principles today may call for a different sort of action.

Scepticism and Criticism

Since the Renaissance, and more particularly since the Enlightenment, world-views have been developed which involve scepticism about basic Christian tenets. Such are the agnosticism which denies that God is knowable, the rationalism which denies that He is incomprehensible, the idealism which denies that He is transcendent, and the existentialism which denies rationality in His relationships with us. When these un- and anti-biblical principles seep into men's theologies at presuppositional level, as today they frequently do, faithful interpretation of Holy Scripture becomes impossible.

Transmission and Translation

Since God has nowhere promised an inerrant transmission of Scripture, it is necessary to affirm that only the autographic text of the original documents was inspired and to maintain the need of textual criticism as a means of detecting any slips that may have crept into the text in the course of its transmission. The verdict of this science, however, is that the Hebrew and Greek text appear to be amazingly well preserved, so that we are amply justified in affirming, with the Westminster Confession, a singular providence of God in this matter and in declaring that the authority of Scripture is in no way jeopardized by the fact that the copies we possess are not entirely error-free.

Similarly, no translation is or can be perfect, and all translations are an additional step away from the *autographa*. Yet the verdict of linguistic science is that English-speaking Christians, at least, are exceedingly well served in these days with a host of excellent translations and have no cause for hesitating to conclude that the true Word of God is within their reach. Indeed, in view of the frequent repetition in Scripture of the main matters with which it deals and also of the Holy Spirit's constant witness to and through the Word, no serious translation of Holy Scripture will so destroy its meaning as to render it unable to make its reader 'wise for salvation through faith in Christ Jesus' (2 Tim. 3:15).

Inerrancy and Authority

In our affirmation of the authority of Scripture as involving its total truth, we are consciously standing with Christ and His apostles, indeed with the whole Bible and with the main stream of Church history from the first days until very recently. We are concerned at the casual, inadvertent, and seemingly thoughtless way in which a belief of such far-reaching importance has been given up by so many in our day.

We are conscious too that great and grave confusion results from ceasing to maintain the total truth of the Bible whose authority one professes to acknowledge. The result of taking this step is that the Bible which God gave loses its authority, and what has authority instead is a Bible reduced in content according to the demands of one's critical reasonings and in principle reducible still further once one has started. This means that at bottom independent reason now has authority, as opposed to Scriptural teaching. If this is not seen and if for the time being basic evangelical doctrines are still held, persons denying the full truth of Scripture may claim an evangelical identity while methodologically they have moved away from the evangelical principle of knowledge to an unstable subjectivism, and will find it hard not to move further.

We affirm that what Scripture says, God says. May He be glorified. Amen and Amen.

APPENDIX II

THE CHICAGO STATEMENT ON BIBLICAL HERMENEUTICS (1982)

In November 1982 the International Council on Biblical Inerrancy called a second international conference of approximately 100 scholars to tackle a second major task, the achieving of a consensus on the principles and practice of biblical interpretation. It was recognized that while belief in the inerrancy of Scripture is basic to maintaining its authority, that belief and commitment have real value only so far as the meaning and message of Scripture are understood. In fact, most of the action in present-day debate about the Bible centres upon questions of interpretation and hermeneutics. For this reason the Inerrancy Council had envisaged a second scholars' 'summit' from the outset, and the two statements on Inerrancy and Hermeneutics will be seen to form a significant pair. Once again it was my privilege to share in drafting the articles and Exposition that follow: documents that secured the broad approval of almost all the participants, and are here reproduced by the Council's permission.

ARTICLES OF AFFIRMATION AND DENIAL

Article I.

We affirm that the normative authority of Holy Scripture is the authority of God Himself, and is attested by Jesus Christ, the Lord of the Church.

We deny the legitimacy of separating the authority of Christ from the authority of Scripture, or of opposing the one to the other.

Article II.

We affirm that as Christ is God and Man in one Person, so Scripture is, indivisibly, God's Word in human language.

We deny that the humble, human form of Scripture entails errancy any more than the humanity of Christ, even in His humiliation, entails sin.

Article III.

We affirm that the Person and work of Jesus Christ are the central focus of the entire Bible.

We deny that any method of interpretation which rejects or obscures the Christ-centredness of Scripture is correct.

Article IV.

We affirm that the Holy Spirit who inspired Scripture acts through it today to work faith in its message.

We deny that the Holy Spirit ever teaches to anyone anything which is contrary to the teaching of Scripture.

Article V.

We affirm that the Holy Spirit enables believers to appropriate and apply Scripture to their lives.

We deny that the natural man is able to discern spiritually the biblical message apart from the Holy Spirit.

Article VI.

We affirm that the Bible expresses God's truth in propositional statements, and we declare that biblical truth is both objective and absolute. We further affirm that a statement is true if it represents matters as they actually are, but is an error if it misrepresents the facts.

We deny that, while Scripture is able to make us wise unto salvation, biblical truth should be defined in terms of this function. We further deny that error should be defined as that which wilfully deceives.

Article VII.

We affirm that the meaning expressed in each biblical text is single, definite and fixed.

We deny that the recognition of this single meaning eliminates the variety of its application.

Article VIII.

We affirm that the Bible contains teachings and mandates which apply to all cultural and situational contexts and other mandates which the Bible itself shows apply only to particular situations.

We deny that the distinction between the universal and particular mandates of Scripture can be determined by cultural and situational factors. We further deny that universal mandates may ever be treated as culturally or situationally relative.

Article IX.

We affirm that the term hermeneutics, which historically signified the rules of exegesis, may properly be extended to cover all that is involved in the process of perceiving what the biblical revelation means and how it bears on our lives.

We deny that the message of Scripture derives from, or is dictated by, the interpreter's understanding. Thus we deny that the 'horizons' of the biblical writer and the interpreter may rightly 'fuse' in such a way that what the text communicates to the interpreter is not ultimately controlled by the expressed meaning of the Scripture.

Article X.

We affirm that Scripture communicates God's truth to us verbally through a wide variety of literary forms.

We deny that any of the limits of human language render Scripture inadequate to convey God's message.

Article XI.

We affirm that translations of the text of Scripture can communicate knowledge of God across all temporal and cultural boundaries.

We deny that the meaning of biblical texts is so tied to the culture out of which they came that understanding of the same meaning in other cultures is impossible.

Article XII.

We affirm that in the task of translating the Bible and teaching it in the context of each culture, only those functional equivalents which are faithful to the content of biblical teaching should be employed.

We deny the legitimacy of methods which either are insensitive to the demands of cross-cultural communication or distort biblical meaning in the process.

Article XIII. We affirm that awareness of the literary categories, formal and stylistic, of the various parts of Scripture is essential for proper exegesis, and hence we value genre criticism as one of the many disciplines of biblical study.

We deny that generic categories which negate historicity may rightly be imposed on biblical narratives which present themselves as factual.

Article XIV. We affirm that the biblical record of events, discourses and sayings, though presented in a variety of appropriate literary forms, corresponds to historical fact.

We deny that any event, discourse or saying reported in Scripture was invented by the biblical writers or by the traditions they incorporated.

Article XV. We affirm the necessity of interpreting the Bible according to its literal, or normal, sense. The literal sense is the grammatical-historical sense, that is, the meaning which the writer expressed. Interpretation according to the literal sense will take account of all figures of speech and literary forms found in the text.

We deny the legitimacy of any approach to Scripture that attributes to it meaning which the literal sense does not support.

Article XVI. We affirm that legitimate critical techniques should be used in determining the canonical text and its meaning.

We deny the legitimacy of allowing any method of biblical criticism to question the truth or integrity of the writer's expressed meaning, or of any other scriptural teaching.

Article XVII.

We affirm the unity, harmony and consistency of Scripture and declare that it is its own best interpreter.

We deny that Scripture may be interpreted in such a way as to suggest that one passage corrects or militates against another. We deny that later writers of Scripture misinterpreted earlier passages of Scripture when quoting from or referring to them.

Article XVIII.

We affirm that the Bible's own interpretation of itself is always correct, never deviating from, but rather elucidating, the single meaning of the inspired text. The single meaning of a prophet's words includes, but is not restricted to, the understanding of those words by the prophet and necessarily involves the intention of God evidenced in the fulfilment of those words.

We deny that the writers of Scripture always understood the full implications of their own words.

Article XIX.

We affirm that any pre-understandings which the interpreter brings to Scripture should be in harmony with scriptural teaching and subject to correction by it.

We deny that Scripture should be required to fit alien preunderstandings, inconsistent with itself, such as naturalism, evolutionism, scientism, secular humanism, and relativism.

Article XX.
We affirm that since God is the author of all truth, all truths, biblical and extra-biblical, are consistent and cohere, and that the Bible speaks truth when it touches on matters pertaining to nature, history, or anything else. We further affirm that in some cases extra-biblical data have value for clarifying what Scripture teaches, and for prompting correction of faulty interpretations.

We deny that extra-biblical views ever disprove the teaching of Scripture or hold priority over it.

Article XXI.
We affirm the harmony of special with general revelation and therefore of biblical teaching with the facts of nature.

We deny that any genuine scientific facts are inconsistent with the true meaning of any passage of Scripture.

Article XXII.
We affirm that Genesis 1-11 is factual, as is the rest of the book.

We deny that the teachings of Genesis 1-11 are mythical and that scientific hypotheses about earth history or the origin of humanity may be invoked to overthrow what Scripture teaches about creation.

Article XXIII.
We affirm the clarity of Scripture and specifically of its message about salvation from sin.

We deny that all passages of Scripture are equally clear or have equal bearing on the message of redemption.

Article XXIV.
We affirm that a person is not dependent for understanding of Scripture on the expertise of biblical scholars.

We deny that a person should ignore the fruits of the technical study of Scripture by biblical scholars.

Article XXV. We affirm that the only type of preaching which sufficiently conveys the divine revelation and its proper application to life is that which faithfully expounds the text of Scripture as the Word of God.

We deny that the preacher has any message from God apart from the text of Scripture.

EXPOSITION

The following paragraphs outline the general theological understanding which the Chicago Statement on Biblical Hermeneutics reflects. They were first drafted as a stimulus toward that statement. They have now been revised in the light of it and of many specific suggestions received during the scholars' conference at which it was drawn up. Though the revision could not be completed in time to present to the conference, there is every reason to regard its substance as expressing with broad accuracy the common mind of the signatories of the statement.

Standpoint of the Exposition

The living God, Creator and Redeemer, is a communicator, and the inspired and inerrant Scriptures which set before us his saving revelation in history are his means of communicating with us today. He who once spoke to the world through Jesus Christ his Son speaks to us still in and through his written Word. Publicly and privately, therefore, through preaching, personal study and meditation, with prayer and in the fellowship of the body of Christ, Christian people must continually labour to interpret the Scriptures so that their normative divine message to us may be properly understood. To have formulated the biblical concept of Scripture as authoritative revelation in writing, the God-given rule of faith and life, will be of no profit where the message of Scripture is not rightly grasped and applied. So it is of vital importance to detect and dismiss defective ways of interpreting what is written and to replace them with faithful interpretation of God's infallible Word.

That is the purpose this exposition seeks to serve. What it

offers is basic perspectives on the hermeneutical task in the light of three convictions. First, Scripture, being God's own instruction to us, is abidingly true and utterly trustworthy. Second, hermeneutics is crucial to the battle for biblical authority in the contemporary church. Third, as knowledge of the inerrancy of Scripture must control interpretation, forbidding us to discount anything that Scripture proves to affirm, so interpretation must clarify the scope and significance of that inerrancy by determining what affirmations Scripture actually makes.

The Communion between God and Mankind

God has made mankind in his own image, personal and rational, for eternal loving fellowship with himself in a communion that rests on two-way communication: God addressing to us words of revelation and we answering him in words of prayer and praise. God's gift of language was given us partly to make possible these interchanges and partly also that we might share our understanding of God with others.

In testifying to the historical process from Adam to Christ whereby God re-established fellowship with our fallen race, Scripture depicts him as constantly using his own gift of language to send men messages about what he would do and what they should do. The God of the Bible uses many forms of speech: he narrates, informs, instructs, warns, reasons, promises, commands, explains, exclaims, entreats and encourages. The God who saves is also the God who speaks in all these ways.

Biblical writers, historians, prophets, poets and teachers alike, cite Scripture as God's word of address to all its readers and hearers. To regard Scripture as the Creator's present personal invitation to fellowship, setting standards for faith and godliness not only for its own time but for all time, is integral to biblical faith.

Though God is revealed in the natural order, in the course of history and in the deliverances of conscience, sin makes mankind impervious and unresponsive to this general revelation. And general revelation is in any case only a disclosure of the Creator as the world's good Lord and just Judge; it does not tell of salvation through Jesus Christ. To know about the Christ of Scripture is thus a necessity for that knowledge of God and communion with him to which he calls sinners today. As the biblical message is heard, read, preached and taught, the Holy Spirit works with and through it to open the eyes of the spiritually blind and to instil this knowledge.

God has caused Scripture so to be written, and the Spirit so ministers with it, that all who read it, humbly seeking God's help, will be able to understand its saving message. The Spirit's ministry does not make needless the discipline of personal study but rather makes it effective.

To deny the rational, verbal, cognitive character of God's communication to us, to posit an antithesis as some do between revelation as personal and as propositional, and to doubt the adequacy of language as we have it to bring us God's authentic message are fundamental mistakes. The humble verbal form of biblical language no more invalidates it as revelation of God's mind than the humble servant-form of the Word made flesh invalidates the claim that Jesus truly reveals the Father.

To deny that God has made plain in Scripture as much as each human being needs to know for his or her spiritual welfare would be a further mistake. Any obscurities we find in Scripture are not intrinsic to it but reflect our own limitations of information and insight. Scripture is clear and sufficient both as a source of doctrine, binding the conscience, and as a guide to eternal life and godliness, shaping our worship and service of the God who creates, loves and saves.

The Authority of Scripture

Holy Scripture is the self-revelation of God in and through the words of men. It is both their witness to God and God's witness to himself. As the divine-human record and interpretation of God's redemptive work in history, it is cognitive revelation, truth addressed to our minds for understanding and response. God is its source, and Jesus Christ, the Saviour, is its centre of reference and main subject matter. Its absolute and abiding worth as an infallible directive for faith and living follows from its God-givenness (cf. II Tim. 3:15-17). Being as fully divine as it is human, it expresses God's wisdom in all its teaching and speaks reliably – that is, infallibly and inerrantly – in every informative assertion it makes. It is a set of occasional writings, each with its own specific character and content, which together constitute an organism of universally relevant truth, namely, bad news about universal human sin and need answered by good news about a particular first-century Jew who is shown to be the Son of God and the world's only Saviour. The volume which these constituent books make is as broad as life and bears upon every human problem and aspect of behaviour. In setting before us the history of redemption – the law and the gospel, God's commands, promises, threats, works and ways, and object-lessons concerning faith and obedience and their opposites, with their respective outcomes – Scripture shows us the entire panorama of human existence as God wills us to see it.

The authority of Holy Scripture is bound up with the authority of Jesus Christ, whose recorded words express the principle that the teaching of Israel's Scriptures (our Old Testament), together with his own teaching and the witness of the apostles (our New Testament), constitute his appointed rule of faith and conduct for his followers. He did not criticise his Bible, though he criticised misinterpretations of it; on the contrary, he affirmed its binding authority over him and all his disciples (cf. Matt. 5:17-19). To separate the authority of Christ from that of Scripture and to oppose the one to the other are thus mistakes. To oppose the authority of one apostle to that of another or the teaching of an apostle at one time to that of his teaching at another time are mistakes also.

The Holy Spirit and the Scriptures

The Holy Spirit of God, who moved the human authors to produce the biblical books, now accompanies them with his power. He led the church to discern their inspiration in the canonising process; he continually confirms this discernment to individuals through the unique impact which he causes Scripture to make upon them. He helps them as they study, pray, meditate and seek to learn in the church, to understand and commit themselves to those things which the Bible teaches, and to know the living triune God whom the Bible presents.

The Spirit's illumination can only be expected where the biblical text is diligently studied. Illumination does not yield new truth, over and above what the Bible says; rather, it enables us to see what Scripture was showing us all along. Illumination binds our consciences to Scripture as God's Word and brings joy and worship as we find the Word yielding up to us its meaning. By contrast, intellectual and emotional impulses to disregard or quarrel with the teaching of Scripture come not from the Spirit of God but from some other source. Demonstrable misunderstandings and misinterpretations of Scripture may not be ascribed to the Spirit's leading.

The Idea of Hermeneutics

Biblical hermeneutics has traditionally been understood as the study of right principles for understanding the biblical text. 'Understanding' may stop short at a theoretical and notional level, or it may advance via the assent and commitment of faith to become experiential through personal acquaintance with the God to whom the theories and notions refer. Theoretical understanding of Scripture requires of us no more than is called for to comprehend any ancient literature, that is, sufficient knowledge of the language and background and sufficient empathy with the different cultural context. But there is no experiential understanding of Scripture – no personal knowledge of the God to whom it points – without the Spirit's illumination. Biblical hermeneutics studies the way in which both levels of understanding are attained.

The Scope of Biblical Interpretation

The interpreter's task in broadest definition is to understand both what Scripture meant historically and what it means for us today, that is, how it bears on our lives. This task involves three constant activities.

First comes *exegesis*, this extracting from the text of what God by the human writer was expressing to the latter's envisaged readers.

Second comes *integration*, the correlating of what each exegetical venture has yielded with whatever other biblical teaching bears on the matter in hand and with the rest of biblical teaching as such. Only within this frame of reference can the full meaning of the exegeted teaching be determined.

Third comes *application* of the exegeted teaching, viewed explicitly as God's teaching, for the correcting and directing of thought and action. Application is based on the knowledge that God's character and will, man's nature and need, the saving ministry of Jesus Christ, the experiential aspects of godliness including the common life of the church and the many-sided relationship between God and his world including his plan for its history are realities which do not change with the passing years. It is with these matters that both testaments constantly deal.

Interpretation and application of Scripture take place most naturally in preaching, and all preaching should be based on this threefold procedure. Otherwise, biblical teaching will be misunderstood and misapplied, and confusion and ignorance regarding God and his ways will result.

Formal Rules of Biblical Interpretation

The faithful use of reason in biblical interpretation is ministerial, not magisterial; the believing interpreter will use his mind not to impose or manufacture meaning but to grasp the meaning that is already there in the material itself. The work of scholars who, though not themselves Christians, have been able to understand biblical ideas accurately will be a valuable resource in the theoretical part of the interpreter's task.

a. Interpretation should adhere to the *literal sense*, that is, the single literary meaning which each passage carries. The initial quest is always for what God's penman meant by what he wrote. The discipline of interpretation excludes all attempts to go behind the text, just as it excludes all reading into passages of meanings which cannot be read out of them and all pursuit of ideas sparked off in us by the text which do not arise as part of the author's own expressed flow of thought. Symbols and figures of speech must be recognised for what they are, and arbitrary allegorising (as distinct from the drawing out of typology which was demonstrably in the writer's mind) must be avoided.

b. The literal sense of each passage should be sought by *the grammatical-historical method*, that is, by asking what is the linguistically natural way to understand the text in its historical setting. Textual, historical, literary and theological study, aided by linguistic skills – philological, semantic, logical – is the way forward here. Passages should be exegeted in the context of the book of which they are part, and the quest for the writer's own meaning as distinct from that of his known or supposed sources, must be constantly pursued. The legitimate use of the various critical disciplines is not to call into question the integrity or truth of the writer's meaning but simply to help us determine it.

c. Interpretation should adhere to the principle of *harmony* in the biblical material. Scripture exhibits a wide diversity of concepts and viewpoints within a common faith and an advancing disclosure of divine truth within the biblical period. These differences should not be minimised, but the unity which underlies the diversity should not be lost sight of at any point. We should look to Scripture to interpret Scripture and deny as a matter of method that particular texts, all of which have the one Holy Spirit as their source, can be genuinely discrepant with each other. Even when we cannot at present demonstrate their harmony in a convincing way, we should proceed on the basis that they are in fact harmonious and that fuller knowledge will show this.

d. Interpretation should be *canonical*, that is, the teaching of the Bible as a whole should always be viewed as providing the framework within which our understanding of each particular passage must finally be reached and into which it must finally be fitted.

Valuable as an aid in determining the literal meaning of biblical passages is the discipline of genre criticism, which seeks to identify in terms of style, form and content, the various literary categories to which the biblical books and particular passages within them belong. The literary genre in which each writer creates his text belongs in part at least to his own culture and will be clarified through knowledge of that culture. Since mistakes about genre lead to large-scale misunderstandings of biblical material, it is important that this particular discipline not be neglected.

The Centrality of Jesus Christ in the Biblical Message

Jesus Christ and the saving grace of God in him are the central themes of the Bible. Both Old and New Testaments bear witness to Christ, and the New Testament interpretation of the Old Testament points to him consistently. Types and prophecies in the Old Testament anticipated his coming, his atoning death, his resurrection, his reign and his return. The office and ministry of priests, prophets and kings, the divinely instituted ritual and sacrificial offerings, and the patterns of redemptive action in Old Testament history, all had typical significance as foreshadowings of Jesus. Old Testament believers looked forward to his coming and lived and were saved by faith which had Christ and his kingdom in view, just as Christians today are saved by faith in Christ, the Saviour, who died for our sins and who now lives and reigns and will one day return. That the church and kingdom of Jesus Christ are central to the plan of God which Scripture reveals is not open to question, though opinions divide as to the precise way in which church and kingdom relate to each other. Any way of interpreting Scripture which misses its consistent Christ-centredness must be judged erroneous.

Biblical and Extra-biblical Knowledge

Since all facts cohere, the truth about them must be coherent also; and since God, the author of all Scripture, is also the Lord of all facts, there can in principle be no contradiction between a right understanding of what Scripture says and a right account of any reality or event in the created order. Any appearance of contradiction here would argue misunderstanding or inadequate knowledge, either of what Scripture really affirms or of what the extra-biblical facts really are. Thus it would be a summons to reassessment and further scholarly enquiry.

Biblical Statements and Natural Science

What the Bible says about the facts of nature is as true and trustworthy as anything else it says. However, it speaks of natural phenomena as they are spoken of in ordinary language, not in the explanatory technical terms of modern science; it accounts for natural events in terms of the action of God, not in terms of causal links within the created order; and it often describes natural processes figuratively and poetically, not analytically and prosaically as modern science seeks to do. This being so, differences of opinion as to the correct scientific account to give of natural facts and events which Scripture celebrates can hardly be avoided.

It should be remembered, however, that Scripture was given to reveal God, not to address scientific issues in scientific terms, and that, as it does not use the language of modern science, so it does not require scientific knowledge about the internal processes of God's creation for the understanding of its essential message about God and ourselves. Scripture interprets scientific knowledge by relating it to the revealed purpose and work of God, thus establishing an ultimate context for the study and reform of scientific ideas. It is not for scientific theories to dictate what Scripture may and may not say, although extra-biblical information will sometimes helpfully expose a misinterpretation of Scripture.

In fact, interrogating biblical statements concerning nature in the light of scientific knowledge about their subject matter may help toward attaining a more precise exegesis of them. For though exegesis must be controlled by the text itself, not shaped by extraneous considerations, the exegetical process is constantly stimulated by questioning the text as to whether it means this or that.

Norm and Culture in the Biblical Revelation

As we find in Scripture unchanging truths about God and his will expressed in a variety of verbal forms, so we find them applied in a variety of cultural and situational contexts. Not all biblical teaching about conduct is normative for behaviour today. Some applications of moral principles are restricted to a limited audience, the nature and extent of which Scripture itself specifies. One task of exegesis is to distinguish these absolute and normative truths from those aspects of their recorded application which are relative to changing situations. Only when this distinction is drawn can we hope to see how the same absolute truths apply to us in our own culture.

To fail to see how a particular application of an absolute principle has been culturally determined (for instance, as most would agree, Paul's command that Christians greet each other with a kiss) and to treat a revealed absolute as culturally relative (for instance, as again most would agree, God's prohibition in the Pentateuch of homosexual activity) would both be mistakes. Though cultural developments, including conventional values and latter-day social change, may legitimately challenge traditional ways of applying biblical principles, they may not be used either to modify those principles in themselves or to evade their application altogether.

In cross-cultural communication a further step must be taken, the Christian teacher must re-apply revealed absolutes to persons living in a culture that is not the teacher's own. The demands of this task highlight the importance of his being clear on what is absolute in the biblical presentation of the will and work of God and what is a culturally relative application of it. Engaging in the task may help him toward clarity at this point by making him more alert than before to the presence in Scripture of culturally conditioned applications of truth, which have to be adjusted according to the cultural variable.

Encountering God Through His Word

The twentieth century has seen many attempts to assert the instrumentality of Scripture in bringing to us God's Word while yet denying that that Word has been set forth for all time in the words of the biblical text. These views regard the text as the fallible human witness by means of which God fashions and prompts those insights which he gives us through preaching and Bible study. But for the most part these views include a denial that the Word of God is cognitive communication, and thus they lapse inescapably into impressionistic mysticism. Also, their denial that Scripture is the objectively given Word of God makes the relation of that Word to the text indefinable and hence permanently problematical. This is true of all current forms of neo-orthodox and existentialist theology, including the so-called 'new hermeneutic', which is an extreme and incoherent version of the approach described.

The need to appreciate the cultural differences between our world and that of the biblical writers and to be ready to find that God through his Word is challenging the presuppositions and limitations of our present outlook, are two emphases currently associated with the 'new hermeneutic'. But both really belong to the understanding of the interpretative task which this exposition has set out.

The same is true of the emphasis laid in theology of the existentialist type on the reality of transforming encounter with God and his Son, Jesus Christ, through the Scriptures. Certainly, the crowning glory of the Scriptures is that they do in fact mediate life-giving fellowship with God incarnate, the living Christ of whom they testify, the divine Saviour whose words 'are spirit and . . . are life' (John 6:63). But there is no Christ save the Christ of the Bible, and only to the extent that the Bible's presentation of Jesus and of God's plan centring upon him is trusted can genuine spiritual encounter with Jesus Christ ever be expected to take place. It is by means of disciplined interpretation of a trusted Bible that the Father and Son, through the Spirit, make themselves known to sinful men. To such transforming encounters the hermeneutical principles and procedures stated here both mark and guard the road.

J. I. Packer

SUGGESTIONS FOR FURTHER READING

(a) Some classical Anglican statements:

'A Fruitful Exhortation to the Reading and Knowledge of
Holy Scripture' in *The Homilies*, Book I (1547); 'An Information for them which take Offence at certain places
of the Holy Scripture' in *The Homilies*, Book II (1571).

Thomas Cranmer: 'A Prologue or Preface . . . (to the Bible)'
(1540) in *Remains and Letters* (Parker Society: Cambridge,
1846), pp. 118-125.

William Goode: *The Divine Rule of Faith and Practice*,
especially Chapter XI, 'The Doctrine of the Church of
England and her principal Divines on the subject of this
work' (London, 2 vols., 1842).

Richard Hooker: *Laws of Ecclesiastical Polity*, especially
Books I. xiii-xxiv, V. xx-xxii (I-IV, 1594; V, 1597). Several
editions printed in the last century at Oxford.

John Jewel: *A Treatise of the Holy Scriptures* (preached,
1570; printed, 1582) in *Works* (Parker Society: Cambridge,
1850), Vol. IV, pp. 1161-1188.

William Whitaker: *A Disputation on Holy Scripture against
the Papists* (1588) (Parker Society: Cambridge, 1849).

Compare also:

John Calvin: *Institutes of the Christian Religion*, especially
Books I. vi-x, IV. viii-ix (1559; English translations available by H. Beveridge and J. T. McNeill).

George H. Tavard: *Holy Writ or Holy Church* (London:
Burns & Oates, 1959). A Roman discussion applauding
some Caroline divines.

(b) Modern views:

(i) Surveys from various standpoints:

Raymond Abba: *The Nature and Authority of the Bible* (London: James Clarke, 1958).

John Baillie: *The Idea of Revelation in Recent Thought* (London: OUP, 1956).

J. Barr: *The Bible in the Modern World* (London: SCM, 1973).

H. D. McDonald: *Ideas of Revelation, an historical study 1700-1860* (London: Macmillan, 1959); *Theories of Revelation, an historical study 1860-1960* (London: Allen & Unwin, 1963).

ed. J. W. Montgomery: *God's Inerrant Word* (Minneapolis: Bethany, 1974).

A. Richardson: *The Bible in the Age of Science* (London: SCM, 1961).

J. D. Smart: *The Interpretation of Scripture* (London: SCM, 1961).

(ii) Individual statements:

Karl Barth: *Church Dogmatics* I/1, I/2, 'The Doctrine of the Word of God' (Edinburgh: T. & T. Clark, 1936, 1956). See also K. Runia: *Karl Barth's Doctrine of Holy Scripture* (Grand Rapids: Eerdmans, 1962).

Emil Brunner: *Revelation and Reason* (London: SCM, 1947). See also P. K. Jewett: *Emil Brunner's Concept of Revelation* (London: James Clarke, 1954).

Rudolf Bultmann: 'The Concept of Revelation in the New Testament' in *Existence and Faith* (writings by Bultmann, selected, translated, and introduced by S. M. Ogden) (London: SCM, 1961), pp. 58-91.

C. H. Dodd: *The Authority of the Bible* (London: Nisbet, 1929, Collins, 1960). Liberal Protestant.

C. Gore: *The Holy Spirit and the Church* (London: John Murray, 1924). Liberal catholic.

Gabriel Hebert: *The Authority of the Old Testament* (London:

Faber, 1947); *The Bible from Within* (London: OUP, 1950).
The 'biblical theology' approach.

(c) Revelation and Inspiration:

G. C. Berkouwer: *General Revelation* (Grand Rapids: Eerd-
mans, 1955); *Holy Scripture* (Grand Rapids: Eerdmans,
1975).
ed. C. F. H. Henry: *Revelation and the Bible* (London: IVP,
1959).
A. Kuyper: *Principles of Sacred Theology* (Grand Rapids:
Eerdmans, 1954). A work of genius.
J. Orr: *Revelation and Inspiration* (London: Duckworth,
1910).
H. Wheeler Robinson: *Inspiration and Revelation in the Old
Testament* (London: OUP, 1946).
B. Vawter: *Biblical Inspiration* (London: Hutchinson, 1972).
Roman Catholic.
B. B. Warfield: *The Inspiration and Authority of the Bible*
(Philadelphia: Presbyterian and Reformed, and London:
Marshall, Morgan & Scott, 1951).
Noel Weeks: *The Sufficiency of Scripture* (London: Banner
of Truth, 1988).
E. J. Young: *Thy Word is Truth* (London: Banner of Truth,
1963).

(d) The Canon of Scripture:

F. F. Bruce: *The Canon of Scripture* (Leicester: IVP, 1988).
R. T. Beckwith: *The Old Testament Canon of the New
Testament Church* (London: SPCK, 1990). Technical.
Bruce Metzger: *The Canon of the New Testament* (Oxford:
OUP, 1987).

(e) Biblical Authority:

ed. J. M. Boice: *The Foundation of Biblical Authority* (Grand
Rapids: Zondervan, 1978).

N. Geldenhuys: *Supreme Authority* (London: Marshall, Morgan & Scott, 1953).

J. I. Packer: *'Fundamentalism' and the Word of God* (London: IVP, 1958).

B. Ramm: *The Witness of the Spirit* (Grand Rapids: Eerdmans, 1959).

Works by Warfield, Kuyper, Hooker, Goode, as cited above.

(f) Biblical Interpretation and Study:

Gordon D. Fee and Douglas Stuart: *How To Read the Bible for all its Worth* (Grand Rapids: Zondervan, 1982).

ed. J. B. Job: *Studying God's Word* (London: IVP, 1972).

ed. I. H. Marshall: *New Testament Interpretation* (Exeter: Paternoster Press, 1977). Technical.

Grant Osborne: *The Hermeneutical Spiral* (Downers Grove: IVP, 1992). Exhaustive.

A. W. Pink: *Profiting from the Word* (London: Banner of Truth, 1970). For self-examination.

R. C. Sproul: *Knowing Scripture* (Downers Grove: IVP, 1977). An excellent introduction.

A. M. Stibbs: rev. D. & G. Wenham, *Understanding God's Word* (London: IVP, 1976). Another excellent primer.

A. C. Thistleton: *New Horizons in Hermeneutics* (London: Marshall Pickering, 1992). Technical.